SOUL MOTHERS' WISDOM

SEVEN INSIGHTS FOR THE SINGLE MOTHER

BETTE J. FREEDSON

PEARLSONG PRESS
NASHVILLE, TN

Pearlsong Press
P.O. Box 58065
Nashville, TN 37205
www.pearlsong.com
www.pearlsongpress.com

© 2014 Bette J. Freedson
www.bettefreedson.com

Book & cover design by Zelda Pudding

Original trade paperback ISBN 9781597190770
Ebook ISBN 9781597190787

The poems "Crossing a Creek" by Martha Courtot and "Peace" by Maryl Willcox are used with permission.

Many of the names in this book have been changed to protect the privacy of the people involved. Events portrayed are true to the best of the author's recollection.

Library of Congress Cataloging-in-Publication Data

Freedson, Bette J., 1943–
  Soul mothers' wisdom : seven insights for the single mother / Bette J. Freedson.
      pages cm
  ISBN 978-1-59719-077-0 (original trade pbk. : alk. paper) — ISBN 978-1-59719-078-7 (ebook)
  1. Single mothers. 2. Single mothers—Psychology. I. Title.
  HQ759.915.F74 2015
  306.874'32—dc23
                                      2014032206

"Bette Freedson has written an enormously useful book on single parenting. As an expert clinician, she has illustrated her suggestions about single parenting with real life clinical cases. But most mportant, she describes her own experiences from shock and despair through adaptation after successful adaptation. This book gives advice and hope to so many overwhelmed parents traveling the same path. A must read!"

JACK WELTNER, MD
child & family therapist, international lecturer on family therapy, author, "A Structural Approach to the Single Parent Family"

"*Soul Mothers' Wisdom* is not your usual 'how to' book. It gives real-life examples of single mothers coping with their situations. In a lovely narrative style and using concise tips, Bette Freedson outlines the steps that individual 'Soul Mothers' took and others can take to succeed as single parents. *Soul Mothers' Wisdom* is both readable and useful."

DR. SELMA MILLER
former president of the NY chapter of the American Association for Marriage & Family Therapists (AAMFT), former member of the National Board of the AAMFT

"Bette Freedson has written a winner in *Soul Mothers' Wisdom*. Her numerous insights and suggestions—gleaned from her own experience as a single mother as well as her years of practicing psychotherapy—are infused with compassion and wisdom. Her goal is to have women not just survive single parenting but instead thrive, and she succeeds wonderfully. *Soul Mothers' Wisdom* is thus the go-to guidebook for anyone navigating these often-confusing and painful waters."

J. WESLEY BOYD, MD, PhD
author, Almost Addicted
faculty member in psychiatry, Harvard Medical School

"As an educator, I particularly found the parenting advice on dealing with stress, building self esteem, and handling misbehavior to be on target and helpful. Single mothers will find this inspirational book to be a valuable resource."

RICH WEINFELD
author, Smart Kids with Learning Difficulties, Helping Boys Succeed in School, School Success for Kids with High Functioning Autism, & Special Needs Advocacy Resource Book

"Bette Freedson has written an empowering and inspiring workbook for the single mother that will serve both as a trusted guide and a wise companion. Every chapter contains useful tips and important questions to reflect upon which, if truly engaged, will foster the psychospiritual evolution of the reader, enabling her to transform the inevitable challenges and hardships of single motherhood into blessings. Freedson has intimate knowledge of the territory of which she writes, both from a personal and professional perspective. This allows her to go directly to the heart of the matter, and inspires trust in the reader. It's hard to continue to feel overwhelmed and alone when you read a book like this; rather you will feel encouraged, as well as connected to Spirit and the human family. Highly recommended."

JUDY TSAFRIR, MD
holistic adult & child psychiatrist & psychoanalyst
faculty member, **Harvard Medical School**

"Bette Freedson provides lucid guidance in the form of a coherent, workable program that shows the reader how to rob the boogey man of his power to scare, victimize and stress women into believing that one person cannot do a two-person job. Self-care is not always easy to come by in the often-harried existence of the single mother. Yet the gentleness of Bette's *yes, you can* and the guidance she provides to an inner oasis can seem attainable. Not only that, but she highlights authenticity in a way that is quite miraculous by showing that meditation as a coping skill can be brought to the even deeper level of trusting intuition....Bette demonstrates how having 'outrageous faith' allows us to find gifts embedded in our problems. She is a role model par excellence, and has written a book hat will be dog-eared by those who are willing to learn and practice what her experience, wisdom, intelligence, humor, kindness and enthusiasm has manifest. This book could pertain to anyone."

HELEN ADRIENNE, LCSW, BCD
author, **On Fertile Ground: Healing Infertility**

"This is a fine book full of support for single parents who have to face the job of raising children alone, and having to share them with another caregiver when they return to work. I would advise all single mothers to read it."

T. BERRY BRAZELTON, MD
Professor of Pediatrics Emeritus at **Harvard Medical School**
developer of the **Brazelton Neonatal Behavioral Assessment Scale**
author of more than 30 books on child development
host of Emmy-award-winning TV show **What Every Baby Knows**

"For twenty-six years I've had a solo general practice of Osteopathic medicine. This has taught me and continues to teach me that the body's inherent mechanism has the wisdom and potency to heal. In *Soul Mothers' Wisdom*, Bette Freedson has given a flexible road map to access this soul's sparkle, the spirit of one's truth, the psychic intuitive wisdom and the realization of inner peace. This is a gift that will last forever and is useful to everyone. It transcends so-called self-help books, for it allows one to see the truth that life's friction gives us direction and is the centripetal force that keeps us on the spiral path."

TIM KINGSBURY, D.O.
Kittery, ME

For my children and my grandchildren.

CONTENTS

ACKNOWLEDGEMENTS
My Gratefulness List Is Long

My children, Laura and Julia: Thank you for being. And thank you for the joy you have brought to my life.

My beloved grandchildren, Ella, Tess, Tovah and Ian: You are the lights of my life.

Ray A., beloved husband: Thank you for being my best friend, my soul companion, and appreciator of my sparkle.

Don F., father of my children and forever partner in loving them: From you I have learned much about forgiveness.

Keith G. and Arturo F., my sons-in-law: Thank you for the love, intelligence, and creativity you bring to our family.

My sister, Gini J., who listens with love and wisdom, and my "brother," Lester "Jack" S., who staunchly supports my endeavors.

Tybee and Irving J, my parents: Thank you for bringing me in, and carving my path.

My cherished Auntie Bea and Uncle Gerry D.

Auntie Bea R., for bringing humor to sadness.

Flora S., "Gummy": Thank you for your divine guidance when I needed it.

Grandpa Ned, my "Papa."

My cousins, Peggy D. and Charlie M., Michael and Robyn D., Gary and Barbie D.

Honey and Eli F.: Thank you for Don.

Janice and Clarence A.: Thank you for Ray.

Roberta and Lloyd G., and Evelyn and Miguel F., my daughters' in-laws: Thank you for sharing your sons, and for the enrichment you bring to our lives.

Oma Gerti Z.: Thank you for your loving strength.

Risa S., my dearest friend: Thank you for your insistence that I follow my path, and for your belief in me to become whole.

Joey S.: Thank you for sharing Risa, and for your wise guidance during difficult times.

Blanche B.: Thank you for being my loyal mentor, inspiring muse, brilliant editor, and cherished friend, and for coaching me, and loving me, through the final years of writing this book.

Bonnie and David W., "Sister and Brother" of my heart: Thank you for supporting me during divorce, for unconditionally loving my girls, and for introducing me to Blanche.

Jeff Z., Ph.D., learned disciple of Milton Erickson, M.D. and world-proclaimed master of Ericksonian hypnosis: Thank you for gently inspiring me to complete my manuscript, and for utilizing your kindness, generosity, skill, and humor to help me grow.

John S., former partner who lovingly helped me through tumultuous years: May your Soul rest in peace.

Jack W., M.D., "The Brevity Man": Respected mentor and friend, master family therapist, author, and self-proclaimed "world's greatest golfer," who has generously read my drafts and lovingly criticized my verbosity.

Elevate Communications: Special thanks to Keith G. and John G. for being there with expertise and understanding.

Larry R., dear friend: Thank you for giving my first private practice a home, a name, and an inspiration.

Sam S. and Fr. Ernest S.

Raymond C.: You are the tops. Thank you for loving me.

Sister Jane H.: Soul sister who has encouraged me to trust my authentic Self, laugh at life's absurdities, and throw out an ugly suit!

Father Alfonse F.: Generous and caring benefactor of my practice at The Listening Place in Lynn, Massachusetts.

Charles A.: Principal and mentor, who taught me to value the skills and strengths of each individual.

Jeff O.: Respected computer guru, who has graciously helped me through many frantic late-night techno-crises.

Ruth S.: Cherished friend and sponsor, who taught me how to put "outrageous faith" in my Higher Power.

James S. of Beauvallon: Thank you for your unflagging belief in me.

Jo N. (thank you for mentoring me!), Joan W., and Fran H.: Super peers and gracious readers of my manuscript, who have encouraged me to tell my story.

All former relatives on the Freedson/Fine sides: You will always be family.

Janie K., my witness to forgiveness.

Vanessa W. and Jeremy, Kathy and Hannah W.: Thank you for being my family.

Anita F.: You taught me how to deal with the deal.

Diane L., who has offerred me the gift of service.

Barbara and David S.: Thank you for helping me transcend tragedy.

Carole S.: Special Services Director of MSAD #35, master teacher. colleague and friend, who has nurtured my work with children and parents.

Debby P.: Thank you for guiding me to begin writing this book.

Michele T.: Thank you for lighting my way into the mystery.

Laura L.F.: Thank you for your encouragement and your beautiful spirit.

Boston University School of Social Work: With special thanks to Trudy Duffy, Josephine Lambert, James Garland, Ralph Kolodney, Louise Lowey and Hubie Jones.

Theresa S. of NASW: My best "pitcher," who believed in my "Tips" and in this book.

The Listening Place, Lynn, MA.

Jewish Community Center of the North Shore, Marblehead, MA: Bea P., Mort and Marilyn A., and all members past and present of the board of directors.

Family and Children's Service of Greater Lynn, Lynn, MA.

Marblehead Community Counseling Center, Marblehead, MA.

Education.com.

Helen A.: Your drum will forever beat in my heart.

Rick M.: Thank you for everything.

Susan D.: Special thanks for *Footprintings*.

Rob S.: Special thanks for your magic.

Father Jim W.: Special thanks for your wisdom.

Sue P.: Special thanks for your caring.

Tobi G.: Thank you for your gentle understanding.

Harriet F.: Thank you for your wit and compassion.

And every member of Dr. Jeffery Zeig's New York City Master Class, and his monthly online master classes.

Carol T., Jonas G. and Bet M. of NASW Massachusetts.

Susan L. and Margery G. of NASW Maine.

June C., Elena E., Judy M., Marla D., Marsha B., Linda R., Lynne and Barry, Nick and Susan, Leah and Albert, Diane and Tom, Ruthie and Paul, Cathie and John, Helen and Otto, Helen and Marc, Joe M., Tina C., Hannah S., Annie K., Wendy P., Ron M., Murray K., Jeannette G., Kathy W., Barbie C., Norman G., Gerry P., Moe and John, Dorothy C., Maryann M., Linda M., Charlene A., Liza E., Beau D., Lisa C., Joanna G., Esther B., Nancy L., Craig G., Kim and Steve B., Roberto F., Harvey M., Malva and Michael, Rabbi Jacobson, Rabbi Ira, Rev. Donna, Sr. Frances.

My stress management groups, my women's groups, and every client I have ever had, for trusting me to bear witness to your maturity, resilience, and strength.

All teachers present and past of Maine School Administrative District (MSAD #35). You are the best there is!

Peggy Elam: A most special and heartfelt thank you for Pearlsong Press.

Thank you to all others who have helped me along my journey. Your names are in my heart.

PROLOGUE

Hope For Your Journey–Heart To Heart

A review of the past 25 years reveals a miracle. Looking back, I believe that events came together with a mysterious synchronicity that brought a scared young woman raising two children on her own into the sacred territory of Soul Mother Wisdom. Single motherhood inspired me to reach inside my Self and pull out previously unimaginable resources of courage, forgiveness, and faith, qualities that prevented me from drowning in bitterness and victim-thinking and enabled me to deal with often-overwhelming odds.

I invite you now to join me in imagining that we are sitting in my old house in Maine, where the Reverend John Thompson lived 250 years ago. Here we can sit by the fire or walk in the gardens, as the parson must have done as he counseled and advised his flock. Here we can speak safely, heart to heart, about what it's like to be a single mother. We can discuss what troubles you, and I will help you discover the amazing resources within your true Self.

Inside you awaits the wisdom that can quiet the turmoil in your single mother Soul and guide you on a journey to maturity, resilience and Self-strength. I will tell you how being a single mother has led me to trust my intuition and the wisdom from my authentic Self. My story and the stories of others will help you believe in yourself and trust that you are whole, that your family is intact, and that you can be a successful single mother.

Along my journey many teachers have appeared. At times their messages have been offered in the disguise of confusion. However, as I have seen my way past obstacles I have understood their lessons more clearly. Greater clarity has made me less likely to waste time wallowing in resentment, insecurity or blame. As you read about my story and "listen" to the stories of other single mothers, I hope you will take inspiration from our experiences and discover the accomplishments in your own life story.

For every role we undertake there comes equal responsibility to accomplish certain tasks. Being a single mother is no different. However, single mothers have an *enormous* amount to accomplish, and the stakes are high—the well-being of your children! To help you apply the insights and strategies you will read about, I have distilled the tasks into seven that I believe are some of the most critical. Please note that they are not the only tasks, and you may discover others that are important to you.

As you make sense of the tender issues that arise, these seven insights will show you how even the most baffling challenges can become opportunities for growing stronger, how problems can be channeled into parenting wisdom, and how fear can transform into faith that you can live a more fulfilling life.

Whatever it is you need accomplish or be able to do, with a little patience and a bit of practice I assure you that you can learn to manage single motherhood successfully. You will be able to replace negative thoughts, manage painful emotions and put faith in your inner wisdom. With the ideas and strategies in the seven insights of *Soul Mothers' Wisdom* you will be able to find gratefulness in your life, enjoy the emotional freedom that comes with forgiveness, and model for your children the blessings of being able to cope with what life deals out.

SEVEN CRITICAL TASKS OF SINGLE MOTHERS

With Soul Mother Wisdom you will be able to:

- Transform insecurities and fears into the faith that you are whole, in or out of a marriage, with or without a partner, and that your single mother household is not broken, but an intact family in which all participate in making it work.
- Take heart from the support and insights you derive from the

stories of other single mothers, allowing their "lessons" of courage to remind you of the strength revealed in your own story, and inspire you to become creatively effective in your parenting and more trusting in the wisdom of your authentic Self.

- Manage your stress and painful feelings while staying emotionally connected to your children, because you understand that your Self management helps them deal with their own stress, emotions and behavior, and empowers their growing resilience and independence.

- Allow your children to remain connected to the other parent and extended family, assuming safety needs are met, while managing any feelings of competition, insecurity or resentment that arise in you, in order to keep from transmitting these negatives to your kids.

- Refrain from using your children (even older ones) as emotional supports, but rather seek appropriate adult/peer support for venting or for emotional working through.

- Use a combination of inner wisdom, a toolkit of positive coping strategies, effective parenting skills, and outside supports to reason through problems and to manage fears and insecurities. When you operate with these resources, you increase the potential to protect your children from excess stress.

- Cope as follows:
    View difficulties as opportunities.
    Assess the effectiveness of coping choices and accept personal responsibility without blaming Self or others.
    Discard strategies that no longer solve your problems.
    Try out new strategies, and seek professional help when you need it.

I hope that you will find courage and inspiration in these pages. I hope that what I have to offer will help you add positive meaning to the chapters of your story. I hope that with this book as guidance and comfort you will recognize your own teachers, their lessons and their gifts, and come to believe that single motherhood can be a journey to maturity, resilience, and strength, as well as to abiding and authentic peace of Soul Mother Wisdom.

INTRODUCTION

Healing, Succeeding and Becoming Wise–The Soul Mother Way

Single motherhood came to my life twice. First when my marriage of thirteen years crumbled, and then a number of years later when my ex-husband died of a heart attack. Even though primary custody of the girls had been mine before he died, being a divorced "widow" added unexpected dimensions to the requirements, responsibilities, and emotions of single motherhood. Divorced, widowed, re-partnered, remarried or totally on my own, I have been a single mother since the day my ex moved out—and in some ways even before. I am proud to say that a major part of my positive Self-identity is that of a strong and resilient Soul Mother.

However, working my way to the "Soul" part has not always been simple or easy, and sometimes not even obvious! As my daughters were growing up there were times when I wondered if I could really raise them into adulthood. Would I be able to make it that far? For a long time I could not imagine it. Would I—could I—survive the trials and worries of each year, or even each day? Although I faced this and many other uncertainties and obstacles, I did manage to keep us reasonably stable, in our home and in our familiar community.

I have had the privilege of watching my daughters grow into adult women who are contributing to society as mothers and as individuals. Along my journey I have been fortunate enough to have a little luck, but "luck" has also come with a *lot* of hard work. My various trials and struggles, as well as my conscious intention to become strong and stable, have taught me how to make more effective choices and how to take better care of myself.

Some of you may also have some good fortune or some lucky breaks, while others may face problems that stretch coping resources to the max. However, the reality is that whatever your material circumstances and whatever supports you have in your life, all mothering requires know-how, courage and wisdom, and single mothering requires all that and more. As life takes you by storm, you need to be able to mobilize support both inside and outside of your Self. You must have the insight and the confidence to make good decisions, even when you are petrified of making the wrong ones.

The good news is this: Being called upon for such a demanding existence has the potential to inspire you to mature into resilience and strength. When you understand the power of your own personal attitudes and beliefs and can learn to mobilize your treasure of inner resources, you will become able to transcend the daily grind and touch down in the sacred domain of Soul Mother Wisdom.

Many life paths can lead to the cultivation of wisdom. Single motherhood has been that path for me, and may be such a path for you. With wisdom you can feel the essential quality and vitality of your spirit. Wisdom teaches you that you have inner guidance for exercising good judgment in your parenting, for making effective personal decisions for your life, and forming a deep, knowing relationship with your authentic Self.

My search for authentic Self, and for soul wisdom, has been fascinating, and continues to this day. Whether coping with my children, my emotions, my finances, my stability (or instability!), my education, or my career, I have needed a strong center of Self from which to operate. Toward that goal, single motherhood has been one of my strongest motivators. Being a single mother has taught me about myself as a mother and about my Self as a woman.

Regardless of the events that have handed you this difficult and awesome job, you have taken on a blessed assignment. I guarantee you that it is possible to fulfill your many challenges with maturity, resilience, strength, and the gifts of Soul Mother Wisdom. If you are a single mother because of abandonment, divorce, death, deployment, or choice, this book is for you. If you feel like a single mother because the largest share of childrearing falls on you, this book is *definitely* for you!

WHO ARE WE?

I have learned a lot about the courageous and resilient women whom society calls single mothers. We are a diverse group of mothers—and grandmothers. We are women whose mates have deserted us for parts unknown, women whose partners are in far corners of a giant world, keeping an unstable peace. We are mothers of children whose fathers have been rendered unavailable by business, emotional disability, illness, divorce or death.

Some of us have chosen to leave our relationships, or to adopt or give birth to a child on our own. Some of us have even made pilgrimages to bring home babies abandoned by other cultures. Whatever the circumstances, we have this in common—we are largely, if not completely, in charge of our children.

We are of every color, race and religion. We are capable, adaptable, and resilient, often discouraged and almost always determined. On the road to greater maturity, we regularly become exhausted and overwhelmed, and sometimes experience exhilaration.

We may have supportive families or we may not. Some of us work, some receive aid, but rich or poor, we strive with whole hearts to do the job of raising our children well. Each of our stories is unique and amazing, embodying the pain and strength from which we can build a foundation for strength and maturity.

Regardless of how we have entered this overpowering and inspiring life, we share a major common denominator—every day of our lives we are working hard with little time for ourselves, even though we need that time badly. We are tired and we are resolute. As we cope with all our circumstances, we strive to solve our problems, create fulfilling lives, and give our children what they need to grow up well. There are times when our bones ache, and times when we vibrate with energy. Always we crave support and long for understanding.

In this book I share my own story as well as the stories of other single mothers. I trust that through these stories you will recognize your own strength and gather Soul Mother Wisdom. Sharing what I have learned about healing, succeeding and becoming wise is a current step in my own journey as a single mother and as a practicing psychotherapist.

I offer you what I have discovered about how to think, how to manage stress effectively, how to make, and trust, your decisions, and how to muster up the inner resources of courage and hope when things seem bleak. I believe that we can do a better job as single mothers and can feel better about our lives when we know ourselves better and know how to cope with what life deals out.

There were no courses in school for how to be a single mother (or a mother in general)! Those of us who follow the Soul Mother way to wisdom still sometimes fly by the seat of our pants, but we are strong and resilient. If we fall, we pick ourselves up and go on, learning from each episode and gaining maturity along the way.

Who but someone who has walked this path can best comprehend what you face? In my therapy office and over coffee with friends, we talk about our trials and struggles. I bear witness to your dedication and your resolve to overcome the difficulties you face as you bring up your children, watch them leave the nest, and adapt to them as adults. Through the beats of my own heart and soul, I feel your weariness and the weight of your burdens. I relish also the joy of your triumphs.

The purpose and promise of Soul Mother Wisdom is this. On this journey, you can learn to appreciate the woman you are and enjoy the life you are living. You will develop an operating base for all occasions. As you evolve into an increasingly wise and successful single mother, you will be guided by an inner strong Self that knows how to think and act in your best interest and the interest of your children.

The difficulties you face as a single mother, when handled with heart and soul, will create the Self that "knows"—the wise woman with a deep sense of who you really are and the insight to know what to do, especially during rough times.

If you choose the Soul Mother way to healing, succeeding and becoming wise, the insights you acquire will help you to cultivate your solid core of true Self, and guide you to parent your children with the care, affection and strength of a resilient, courageous and wise single mother.

Relax and Read—Using This Book Your Way

When I first became a single mother, and all along the way, I have longed for other single mothers to understand my struggles and help light my way. When you feel overwhelmed and wish for understanding in a world that seems to race by in coupled-ness and frenzy, I hope this book will be a voice of support and sisterhood for you, a beacon of hope to get you through the night—and through every day.

You might choose to read in a linear way, cover to cover, or you may find that waiting on your bedside table there are comforts and insights that can get you through a long twenty-four hours. At the end of each chapter you will find Tips For Understanding, Ideas For Reflection and Insight, and Pages for Journaling. The intention is to make this your personal book, where you can write about the stories of your life, the moments in your day, the fears in the middle of the night, and the wisdom that guides your journey.

My dear sisters, we all need to find positive meaning in the stories we are living. I hope that as you read you will come to see the wisdom and inner strength in the chapters of your stories. It is my passionate dream that as you do the most important job on the planet, this book will inspire you to discover your own authenticity and positive Self-identity as you build your maturity, resilience and strength.

As you live out whatever hands you are dealt, may you find the strength within your true Self. May you live peacefully with a heart full of gratefulness, forgiveness, and faith. May you parent with confidence in the success of your purpose. And may your inner spirit sparkle with the wisdom that resides in your Soul.

INSIGHT ONE

Your Story Reveals Amazing Strength and Soul Wisdom

"I have learned how difficult and rewarding mothering is, and how strong full-time single mothers need to be. Wisdom comes as you look back on experience. I have gained self-respect and confidence in myself. I now have faith that I can be strong, loving and wise for my children and myself."

SINGLE MOTHER CIRCA 2006

OUR AMAZING STORIES

Single mothers, whatever our circumstances, have stories that are uniquely personal, poignantly similar, and wholly amazing. Each story reveals a wealth of parenting wisdom and coping strength that may surprise you. In your story can be seen the ways in which you have trusted your know-how, placed faith in the guidance of a Higher Power, and been empowered by your soul intuition. While no two story lines are exactly the same, the common denominators of responsive resilience, Self-strength and soul wisdom exist in virtually every story. These powerful qualities inspire hope for all single mothers who are doing, and have done, this incredible job.

Consider this: Have you heard or read about a single mother whose devotion and steadfast dedication to her children has encouraged you? Have you been inspired by the story of a single mother whose intuition has helped her overcome difficult circumstances? Perhaps a story about a well-known single mother has made you more appreciative of your own resilience. Or maybe reading about the successful child of a single mother has given you the "If-she-can-do-it, I-can-do-it" brand of parenting motivation. Whatever your experience, you can derive hope from knowing that down through the ages single mothers have survived and succeeded with amazing strength and inner soul wisdom.

Single motherhood did not begin with the "Me-Me-Me" culture of the 1960s and '70s, when divorces increased and the stigma associated with divorce went down. Single mothers have been rearing their children, making ends meet, and attempting to make a good life for their families (and themselves!) since pre-Her-storic times. The stories of these women show us that it is possible to survive in the most challenging situations. Like us, our foremothers must have felt frightened, fragmented and frustrated when illness, wars, and sociocultural or catastrophic changes and events removed them from a partner, demanding virtually superhuman efforts to balance the requirements of children, home and Self.

While we can learn a lot from the heroic stories of past and current single mothers, you might find that you can learn the most about your Self by reflecting on the strength and wisdom in your own life story.

Please bear in mind, however, that while you cannot change what has happened in your life, it is important to allow yourself to feel whatever you feel about what you cannot change. Many single mothers have experienced a great deal of emotional pain. Feeling and accepting that pain, be it sadness, anger, fear, or other feelings, is a crucial step in the process of understanding your Self and coming to experience peace of mind.

Giving yourself permission to feel how you feel allows you to move forward in your emotional progress and supports the integration of your whole, authentic Self. When you become aware of your emotional responses to life's events you can choose how you understand the significance of both the events themselves and your feelings about them. By reviewing, and in some cases, revising the way you view your story, you can choose your actions more thoughtfully in the present and in the future.

Life will always provide opportunities for revising old perspectives and assessing new situations. All you have to do is to recognize your opportunities as they come, be present to the potential for the healing they offer, and make a conscious decision about how to think about it all. The more opportunities for changing perspective you grasp, the stronger you can grow as a parent and as a person. Even when you are stressed, you will be able to move more easily to a wise inner place that can help to heal your pain and increase the inner resources of your authentic Self.

Now, let me tell you how I was taken by surprise by one such opportunity for reassessing my story. This happened a few years ago at a birthday party for my childhood friend.

PERSPECTIVE RE-VIEWED AND REVISED

As children, Lydia and I had played out our imagined "somedays," which included getting married, having children, and "living happily ever after." Many years later, at a birthday party for Lydia during which her children presented a slide collage of her life, I was struck by the contrast between Lydia's "someday" and my own. Our stories had started out similarly—marrying young, becoming teachers, and "retiring" to have babies. But from there our paths diverged, and what followed was quite different.

There in scene after scene I saw a beaming Lydia surrounded by her first (and only) husband and her three devoted children. As I watched my old friend's "happily ever after" on the screen, a video of my "who am I after divorce?" simultaneously played on my mental screen, causing a familiar sadness to tighten around my heart.

My slide show would show me at just 22 years of age marrying a man I liked well enough, thought I loved, and believed was the right man for me. In the next slide I would be 30, caring for a husband who was recovering from a major heart attack and providing virtually full-time care for two babies. In the next slide I am 34, separated, feeling abandoned, and struggling to manage life as a single mother. The next several slides show me in my 40s, bringing up two daughters whose father had died.

In contrast to Lydia surrounded by her loving, "intact" family, I look alone, overtired, stressed out and falling apart. For a few moments, feeling sorry for myself, I wallowed in this sad and sour time warp. When I returned from my melancholy reverie, it startled me to realize

27

how quickly a negative view of my story could break into my thoughts and bring on the old pain. Amazing how fast I could get lost in an old negative vision of my life, and how important to remember that the old version was not, and is not, the whole story of my story.

While it will ever be true that the years of single mothering were hard, I would not want to change a single chapter of my single mother story; for it was also true that during those years of struggle I began to grow up and discover what made up my authentic Self. I developed unique relationships with each of my daughters, and came to see our family of three as a whole unit with relatives and friends who added zest to our lives. The need to achieve financial security and emotional stability had motivated me to develop what had become a fulfilling career.

Now my girls were grown and launched, and despite the old realities I had a good life that included fulfilling work, a successful second marriage, and more wisdom than I had started out with. My girls were doing well, and I was doing well. We had come through okay. Had my life gone as Lydia and I had dreamed, I might not have become the Self that I have become.

Yes, it was true that in those central days of single motherhood I often felt frustrated, frightened, and lonely. But it is just as true that I faced experiences and managed difficulties that strengthened me and increased my ability to access Soul Mother Wisdom for dealing with new realities of my life.

THE POWER OF YOUR STORY: STRENGTH AND WISDOM

While it is normal to have old hurts triggered, it is also possible to allow a more realistically balanced story to live beside the sad one. All the versions of your story have truth to them; it is up to you to decide which version you want to think about at any given time.

Through thoughtful reflection of what you have gone through, it is possible to shift into a more positive meaning and understanding of your story. A perspective shift can help you make more effective choices, change behavior patterns that no longer work, and try new parenting and living strategies that might be more successful. The potential to view your story in a new light is a power-filled tool for consolidating strength and increasing wisdom.

One effective way to shift the "reading" of your story is to refocus thoughts away from fear, anger, and resentment, or painful perspectives, toward thoughts of accomplishments, even small ones. Thinking about the times you have managed difficulties, no matter how insignificant they may seem, can free you from dwelling in negatives, create the calm you crave, and increase your supply of Soul Wisdom.

Choosing to remind yourself that even if you don't *feel* strong, you *are* strong can help you face your challenges one day at a time. Remember this: You are doing the best you can, and your best is good enough!

Following is an affirmation that I regularly used (and still do!) to remind myself of the strength and wisdom in my own story. You might want to use this affirmation when you reflect on your story.

> *I affirm my accomplishments and my resilience. I open my mind and heart to opportunities for growing stronger, and the experiences that move my children toward success. My story continues to offer lessons about living and loving. I can choose how I think about my life as I make the best choices I can for myself, and my children. Every day in every way I am growing into wisdom.*

I realize that now you might be thinking, "Hindsight is easy, but how can I know I'll be okay when I can't see what's ahead?" My reply is this: Yes, hindsight might be easier than seeing what you can't foresee, but hindsight can also be helpful. In reviewing your past circumstances, you realize how strong and resilient you have been. That realization, along with acknowledgement of your accomplishments, can provide you with hope for going forward. However, please bear in mind that it is normal and okay for painful feelings and frustrations to come up. All you need to do is have faith that as you lift yourself out of negative perspectives, you can be better prepared to cope with your life, and more aware of the guidance from your inner Self.

HEROINES

During the hardest years of single mothering, I longed to hear (and still do!) the stories of other single mothers. The experiences, problems and triumphs of strong women like Queen Esther and Norene have inspired me. Even in my own family there are inspirational stories, like that of my Great-Aunt Leona, who brought up her brothers and sisters after their parents died, or the story of my own mother, widowed at 57 and left to manage a business and provide emotional support to two young adult daughters. My guess is that Leona and my mother never used the term "single mother," but the shoe fit even if they didn't wear it! Amazing single mothers like these, and so many others, are my heroines.

While heroines in mythical stories are allowed to employ superhuman qualities and magic to overcome problems, we modern single mother heroines are called upon regularly to slay a "dragon" or two with our weapons of parenting skill, inner strength and Soul Mother Wisdom. Our own rough and tumble realities whirl us into experiences we never could have imagined, and motivate us to call upon resources as amazing as any action heroine ever invented.

Two of my modern heroines, Norene and Queen Esther, have very different personal stories, but both stories reveal common denominators of resilience, strength, and inner wisdom. You will be inspired by ways in which each mother finds herself parenting without the support of a mate. As you read their stories, notice the strength and wisdom that is revealed as each heroine bravely faces single motherhood in her own amazing way.

NORENE'S STORY

Originally, Norene came into psychotherapy to figure out how to deal with her husband's depression. Due to her husband John's deepening emotional despair, Norene had been managing everything related to her children virtually alone for about five years. She came exasperated and exhausted and desperately wanting to find a way to make her husband better. Soon Norene came to realize that it was actually her own life that needed attention.

As we began Norene's therapy, she related an early story of success and a later story of reversal. For many years, Norene and her husband had owned a lucrative but high-maintenance general store. The business had supported them and their two children well, but ultimately the pressure of it became too much for them. Believing that life would be easier without the stress of the business, they sold it at a time when they could turn a nice profit. They invested the money for their children's college education and put some away for the proverbial nest egg.

With money in the bank and less on their minds, Norene and her husband planned that Norene would continue teaching and John would find a job. They would watch their son play baseball, send both kids to college, and enjoy the bounty and leisure of their new life. Circumstances, however, did not go as planned. Surprisingly, Norene's husband remained unemployed during years in which reverses in the economy ate away at their savings. As time went on John fell into despair, while Norene worked harder and became increasingly confused, frustrated, and frightened.

Norene's husband did attempt other businesses, but eventually all failed. He applied for jobs that didn't materialize, and became increasingly morose and dysfunctional. Over time Norene became the front line for supporting the family, making decisions, taking care of children's needs, and trying to shore up her husband's decreasing self-esteem. Norene felt depleted, sad, and angry. She was carrying almost every aspect of their life alone.

Finally John became suicidal and was hospitalized, following which he was treated with a series of shock treatments. Those attempts at curing the depression succeeded only in reducing John's already limited ability to function. Now he became merely a body in the house, unable to manage the smallest task or even think beyond the next half hour. Norene was at her wits' end with exhaustion from taking care of the enormous responsibilities of life's details, including John's medical appointments and regimen. Some women would have bailed, but Norene didn't want to leave him. She had never wanted to be a single mother. In fact, she had always dreaded the idea. But at this point, as John became less able to function as a partner and parent, Norene appeared to be becoming what she had feared the most.

Now, besides the enormity of just plain doing, Norene was starting to face her children's concerns about their emotionally absent father and his ongoing emotional decline. They were aware that their mother was often at the end of her energy rope, and they had questions. "When is dad going to get better?" "Why can't dad visit this college with us?" "I saw daddy in the stands, but why wasn't he watching my game?" "How long are you going to have to support us? When will daddy get a job?"

Despite her weariness and occasionally frantic approach to all she had to do, Norene was not crumbling. In fact, she was actually handling these questions and her enormous responsibilities reasonably well. She answered questions without putting John down, and she was able to say "I don't know" without shame, without blame, and without falling apart in the process.

Norene was learning that although she couldn't make John better, she could forge ahead for the sake of her children. Nevertheless, doubt and fear hung over Norene like a thick industrial smog from which she could not escape. Despite the fact that we continued to discuss a variety of strategies to alleviate her mental and emotional burdens, we couldn't seem to come up with an approach that would effectively relieve Norene's misery

As we went on, it occurred to me that Norene was wrestling with many of the same issues that single mothers face—the exhaustion, the never-ending work, the agonizing worries about money, the flagging energy, and the dilemma of having no ability to change the absent or uninvolved other parent. However, when we discussed options, one of which one was to leave John, Norene would express horror at the possibility of becoming a single mother. Fortunately, my own intuition and Norene's negative view of single motherhood inspired me to try a different approach.

"Norene, you know you have already become, in effect, a single mother!" I ventured during one session.

"I'm *not* a single mother!" Norene countered. "My life is tough, but I am a *married* woman. John is a good man. He was a very good breadwinner until we decided to sell the business and he couldn't find work. Anyway, how could I leave him when he's so depressed? I still love him...I think I do. It's not so easy to tell anymore, but I know that I'm not ready to be a single mother. Besides, wouldn't being a single parent be bad for the children?"

"The bottom line issue here is not whether you stay or go," I told Norene. "Your role as a mother and your responsibility to yourself are constants. It is up to you to make your own life as fulfilling as possible, and you are never going to stop doing your best for your kids. When you stop fighting the truth and accept that you are virtually a single mother, you might be able to see how courageously you've been coping. You've always been frightened of becoming a single mother, but you had no control over the life circumstances that have essentially made you one.

"You are in essence parenting your children alone now," I continued, "and despite the stress of having their father be so depressed, you appear to be doing a damn good job. You already have all the responsibility for the children. Maybe it would help relieve your frustration if you could see that you're living as a single mother, and began to understand that you and your children can survive and have good lives even if their father is unavailable and unable to help. You know, you don't have to leave John to believe that. Can you accept that neither your fulfillment as a woman or your success as a mother are dependent on your husband's emotional condition—or your marital status?"

"I don't know." Norene answered. "But I want to believe it, and I want to understand how I can have a good life when it seems like all I have is hard work and stress."

Once Norene understood that I was not suggesting she leave John, she and I had many ongoing variations of the single mother discussion. We talked about how for hundreds of years single mothers have been strong women. We talked about Norene's successful management of her children's affairs. As Norene began to identify herself as a single mother, she opened to the idea that she could also make a satisfying life for herself and take good care of her children simultaneously.

With this resolve, Norene committed herself to exploring what it would really mean to see herself as a woman with a strong and solid sense of Self. I suggested that we look further into her personal story to understand the roots of her determination to stay in her marriage, while actually operating as if she were a single mother.

We discovered that marriage and motherhood had been Norene's mother's way of life, and embodied what Norene had always believed her life would be. In Norene's family tree we found no models of women who had been single with children. Norene currently knew women who were divorced, but the ones who were single mothers complained about their hardships and disappointments. They would tell her how difficult it was to be a single mom, and Norene was desperately afraid she would end up like them—miserable, lonely, alone.

Over time, Norene reluctantly and somewhat gratefully began to see that like some of these single mothers she struggled, but also like others she was competent and able, prevailing over tough circumstances. I pointed out that her children were adjusting, that she was excelling at her teaching job and managing her husband's complex regimen of medical appointments and treatments. I suggested that she begin to make a life for herself, perhaps plan evenings out with friends, something she had not done since she and John stopped socializing some years before. Norene was open to this idea, and committed herself to exploring the creation of a personal life of her own.

As she continued in therapy, Norene came to know a part of her that was steadfastly married, a part of her that was fearful of being a single mother, and another part of her that was *proud* to be a single mother. As Norene began to integrate these parts, she began to see her story in a new light, and her hopelessness began to subside. Honoring her courage as well as her fear and frustration helped Norene to understand how the choices she made every day kept her from feeling like a victim, and affirmed her resilience.

Norene started to recognize where in her life she had control and where she did not. She agreed to look for something uplifting and fulfilling in her story every day. This was a choice she could control. By accepting the reality of her situation, Norene could look at her story with a fresh vision and see her inner strength. For the first time, the notion of being a single mother was giving Norene a sense of accomplishment, competence, and pride.

As she became more comfortable seeing herself in the single mother role, Norene began to experience less frustration and a new sense of fulfillment. Despite ongoing difficulties, Norene decided to stay married and still do what single mothers do—everything. Accepting her conscious choice enhanced Norene's Self-esteem. No longer did she have to pretend that she was a normally, happily married woman. Norene was more authentically a single mother who was learning that she knew how to handle the rigors of that life.

When I last spoke to Norene, her sense of identity had morphed from seeing herself as a disappointed woman in a failed relationship with a sick man to a woman who could choose how she wanted to live her own life. The children, now a senior in college and a junior in high school, were showing no signs of coming apart emotionally.

Largely because of Norene's sensitivity, her son and daughter had made progress in accepting and adapting to their father's incapacitation. Although sometimes still furious and exasperated, Norene neither painted their father as a villain nor kept the truth of his unremitting illness from the kids. As a result they were showing resilience and empathy in their own endeavors, clearly benefitting from the positive changes their mother was making. Norene's authentic Self was offering her children a fountain of strength. Norene was creating and living a personal story of Self-empowerment, acceptance and peace. Norene was becoming a very wise woman.

QUEEN ESTHER'S STORY

"I'm 83, and I just left my husband of 30 years!"
That was how Esther introduced herself. Believing that at 83 she could still have a future, Esther wanted to understand why she had spent thirty years with a second husband she didn't love. Esther had the wisdom to realize that regardless of her age, at this critical point in her story it was important for her to understand the larger span of her life in order to accept her choice to leave her marriage.

As Esther's story unfolded, it became clear that her understanding and acceptance of her current choices had everything to do with looking at choices in an earlier part of her story. Long before there were social supports and the stigma had faded, Esther had been a single mother. Understanding the impact and meaning of her young single motherhood would hold a key to the answers, and the comfort, that Esther was seeking.

I learned that Esther had married her first husband in the early 1940s, shortly before he entered the service and when Esther "was too young to know what love was." The new husband had come home on leave and left Esther pregnant. Esther's husband was not pleased with this news. When he told her that he wanted her to have an abortion, she agreed that it was a good idea. "And I did have one," she says triumphantly. "It was him!"

After divorcing her husband, Esther found herself a single mother of a small son. In those days of the mid 1940s widows, especially war widows, had some acceptance as single mothers, but divorced single mothers were not as socially accepted. How had Esther coped with her status? What had been her resources? Even so many years later Esther did not fully comprehend how strong she had been to grapple with the social context of the day, and the difficulties that single mothers had faced.

As single mothers in every era must, Esther had to raise her child while dealing with her own emotions. During her son's early childhood, Esther called upon inner and outer resources. She relied on her parents to take care of her little boy while she worked long hours, often traveling alone overnight for her sales job. Esther remained mindful and grateful of the help she was receiving from her family, refusing to see herself as a victim, but rather cultivating an attitude of acceptance that gave her the courage to keep going. Despite her past successes, Esther didn't fully realize the many ways her strength and resilience had helped her so long ago, or understand that these same qualities could help her now.

"Esther," I asked, "wasn't it terribly hard to be a single mother in those days?"

"Yes, it was," she assured me. "I did what I had to do, but there were others harder up than I was, with no families to help."

"What is the secret of this positive attitude you had?" (She still had it into her nineties!)

"I believe in God," she said unhesitatingly. "This was the path He chose for me, and I had to accept that. I felt grateful to have my son. He was so precious, and my mother and father loved him as if he was their own. I accepted my decision to divorce and trusted that this was what God wanted for me. So, you see, I was lucky."

As Esther continued to examine her life story, she came to realize that more than luck had been at work. She was able to recognize the courage and intuitive wisdom that had given her the strength to banish husband number one. Finally she could entertain the idea that there had also been wisdom in her choice to marry husband number two. At a point where she no longer had family support, was weary from her grueling job, and had no financial base, Esther had married a man who could, and would, support her and her son.

Comforted by knowing that her choices had been logical and had stemmed from positive intentions, Esther became more able to make sense of her past experiences and losses, including the death of the young man who had been her only true love. Now, so many years later, ready and able to look back and see her success as a single mother, Esther was engaged in a review that allowed her to know how her coping and survival had been directed by her Soul Mother Wisdom.

Realizing her courage was helping Esther to see the way in which her decision to leave her current husband was also coming from a wise part of her Self. She knew what was right for her now, even as she had known what was right in the past. As Esther achieved these insights, her feelings of sadness, disappointment, and self-doubt began to be replaced by a sense of well-being and appreciation for Soul Mother Wisdom.

Through all her losses and disappointments Esther had kept her sense of humor, her belief in God, and the persistent effort to give her son a good life. She maintained her dedication to him even to the day when, as a grown man, he asked for her blessing to follow his destiny 3000 miles away. "My heart broke," she told me. "But what could I say? This is what he wanted, and I wanted him to be happy."

When asked how I should identify her in my book, Esther requested that she be called "Queen Esther." Partly, she says, because Queen Esther in the Bible was a wise woman and a survivor, and partly because she saw herself as a modern queen, courageously having raised a boy into a good man. It meant the world to Esther to understand that strong and wise parts of herself had guided her so many years ago, and could continue to guide her now. She had always made choices from a truth inside that directed her to do the right thing. Queen Esther was then, and will ever be, a true Soul Mother.

Norene's story and Queen Esther's story are only two of many amazing stories of single mothers. As you live your own story with its highs, its lows, the characters, the conflicts, and the resolutions, you, too are creating a story of courage and meaning. In your own personal story, as well as in the stories of other single mothers, you will find the inspirations for healing and succeeding and becoming wise.

YOU, TOO ARE A HEROINE

As you face the day-to-day grind of life and the enormous challenge of being a single mother in today's world, remember that you, too, have an inspiring story. In your own story you can discover the strengths that will remind you to appreciate the heroine that you are.

A short few years ago a once-popular song offered the idea that "what's too painful to remember we simply choose to forget." Indeed, there is a part of the psyche that wants to forget pain, but there is also a part of us that wants to, and often tries to, remember. It is generally accepted by mental health professionals that although attention to the past may bring up painful memories, when handled carefully and safely, *the way out is through.*

As you review your story, be gentle with yourself. Sometimes intense emotions can rise up and surprise you like the shadowy pictures of the Loch Ness monster. But like the threat of a mythical monster, the threat of painful emotions is only as real as you believe it to be. The healthy truth is that in some circumstances it is in the service of recovery to review upsetting material, while in other circumstances it is advisable to refrain. For those single mothers with highly traumatic past events, "working through" may best be done in a safe setting with a trusted therapist or clergy person. Whatever you want to do, the choice is yours.

But in whatever way you choose to focus—or not focus—on past (or current) events, deriving positive meanings from your story can help you create a more positive view of your life and learn more effective ways to deal with stressors now and in the future. If and when you're willing to engage in the self-examination process, your story can offer you jewels of insight about the skills you have, those you wish to develop, and the nature of your authentic Self.

Please remember this: Being a strong single mother does not mean that you are some superwoman who must relive every painful moment, bear everything alone, or do everything perfectly. There may be some days—even in the midst of growing stronger—that you may not want to think about personal growth or Self-examination. Maybe you just want to cry for a while, or sit and stare into space hoping to be rescued. Wisdom allows you to know when to move forward and when to stay put.

Guided by the wisdom you derive from the stories of others and from your own story, you will find the insight to overcome difficulties, resolve problems, and transcend negative emotions. As time goes on you will begin to make more of your decisions out of the peace that comes from love, forgiveness, and faith in your own inner guidance.

TIPS FOR UNDERSTANDING: FINDING POSITIVE MEANING IN YOUR STORY

"We tell ourselves certain stories for a reason, " Joshua Lang pointed out in his 2013 *New York Times Magazine* article "Unintentional Motherhood." As Katie Watson, a bioethicist at Northwestern University's Feinberg School of Medicine, explained to Lang, "It's psychologically in our interest to tell a positive story and move forward."

Tip One

Even when life is packed with things to do and problems to face, taking the time to reflect upon your own story can be a path to self-acceptance and contentment. As you notice what thoughts and feelings arise, you can recognize the significance and important meanings in your story. This awareness can assist you in making more conscious decisions and choices.

Tip Two

As you live your story, you may notice negative thoughts going through your mind from time to time. There is no need to reject them, or try to hold them. Just notice them and allow them to be. You might ask yourself, "How am I perceiving what has happened in my life right now?" If you choose to, you can change the negative channel in your mind and focus instead on ways in which you have exhibited strength, courage and resilience. You have a choice about how to view your story, including what is happening in your life right now.

Tip Three

As a daily practice, spend a few moments consciously focusing on your new view. If you can find even a small kernel of truth in seeing things a more positive way, you can put this more uplifting version of your story alongside the old negative one. When stressors trigger the old sad, sour emotions, you can manage the feelings by reminding yourself that you have another choice about how to view circumstances. Practice may not make perfect, but it will help you stay more peaceful and have more trust in your ability to use your inner wisdom.

Tip Four

When seeing the positives feels too hard, or you feel too discouraged, you can seek the support of a trusted friend, another single mother, a clergy person, or a mental health professional. Discussing your story with a compassionate other can help you see a more balanced view. While validating your pain is always important, sharing your story with a safe person can help you to notice where there is enlightenment instead of darkness, where there is strength instead of weakness, and where your own inner wisdom can give you the hope that will brighten your spirit.

Tip Five

Some single mothers find it helpful to join a support group of other mothers whose stories can provide new perspectives that may help to see your story in a new light. Shared stories of strength and hope can inspire you to see the wisdom in your own story. It might be helpful to remember that you can learn to accept your feelings, find support for them, and be able to act in ways that can lead to the best outcomes for yourself and your children.

You can now affirm:

With inspiration and comfort from the support and hope of other single mothers' stories, I find the will and courage to overcome my problems. I can find insight and wisdom within myself to guide my amazing journey.

IDEAS FOR REFLECTION AND INSIGHT: YOUR PERSONAL STORY

You might like to take a moment now or later to relax and think about your life story. It could be just before falling to sleep, or just before getting up in the morning. During those quiet moments you can allow negative thoughts and emotions to move gently out of the way. As you reflect on the past, on the present, and on your hopes and desires for the future, simply allow all thoughts to come in and go out, trusting that the insights you need will come to you now or may come later. You can affirm the following statement:

Negative thoughts will have no negative effect on me.

As part of your reflection, you might also consider the following questions:

What insights have I gained from the stories of others?

What significant events come to mind from my own story? What can I learn from how I handled these events?

Who are the people from whom I have gathered strength and learned important lessons?

Where have my inspirations come from?

In what ways have those inspirations helped me to live life with more strength and peace?

Is there a problem I face now that could be more easily solved by using some of the inspirations and wisdom that I have gathered?

What choices have I made to solve past problems?

In what situations have I used inner wisdom to solve problems?

Has there been a gift from adversity that I did not recognize in its time, but that now I can see as a positive influence in my life?

What are the gifts in the difficulties I now face?

You can use the following exercise to make sense of your story and access the strength and wisdom within your Self.

Take a gentle breath, and as you exhale, feel into the truth of your strength and wisdom. Affirm that you are growing in just the right way for you.

Now take a moment to sense how much you have accomplished. Accept whatever comes to you, whether or not it makes sense in the moment. If negative thoughts come in, just let them come and go. There is no need to hold them, or to push them away. Notice what you feel, and come back to your breath.

You can begin to notice how many perspectives to your story there are. You are in charge of your choice of perspective.

You can allow insight to be your guide and help you understand the amazing strength and Soul Wisdom of your story.

PAGES FOR JOURNALING

While it is always a challenge for a busy single mother to find time for herself, taking even five minutes to think or write about something meaningful can open the door to wisdom and peace.

For those of you new to journaling, as well as for those of you to whom journals are beloved friends, this might be a good time to take a moment to sit quietly, reflect upon your own life story so far, and jot down your insights in your own personal way.

Writing can clear the mind and open insights that reveal strength and wisdom. Like many of us, you may find that awareness comes through the mind like a beam of light that soon fades, or like a dream that is vivid and quickly forgotten. When you write down your thoughts, you can retrieve them when you want or need them.

Of course, it's okay if you choose not to write. The wise knowing remains inside, waiting for you to access its gifts any time you decide to listen to the guidance that comes from your own inner voice of Soul Mother Wisdom.

INSIGHT TWO

With a Solid Self and Soul Wisdom You Can Be Okay

"Who am I? Jon's mom. Rebecca's mom. I am a daughter, and a sister, a niece, an aunt, a cousin. God willing, one day to be a grandmother. For 23 years I thought of myself as half of a couple—one side of the coin. At age 40 the question became 'What does the whole of me look like?' Me. Me. My. My. With arms open, heart open, spirit free, exposed, beautiful, graceful, healthy, strong. Trust. Peace. Release. My mind. My body. My soul. My heart. My spirit. Inside is the lovely, lively, vibrant, WHOLE of ME. Love! Self!"

SINGLE MOTHER, CIRCA 2007

DESTINATION WHOLENESS: I DISCOVER MY TRUE COLORS

Discovering more about your whole Self can happen in surprising ways. When you are open to the clues and the conclusions you can become more solid, develop greater soul wisdom, and find that you can be okay in all sorts of situations.

An occasion of unexpected growth happened to me a number of years ago. Never could I have guessed that it would be in the land of make believe, fantasy and fake that I was destined to discover my true colors and find out more about my wholeness. Let me tell you how it all happened.

The destination was Hollywood, California and Zeke's big birthday party. The cousin of my ex-husband, Dov, Zeke was also the best friend of my then-boyfriend, a psychiatrist who loved L.A. as much as he loved Zeke. Zeke had his fifteen minutes of fame as a supporting actor in a 1984 award-winning movie. His wife, Nina, a former chorus girl, was making a successful career out of preserving her looks.

"It'll be a blast!" insisted Zeke's sister, my close friend Joyce. "My brother knows everyone! Big names will be there—Danny, and maybe Michael, and definitely Fran" (pre-*The Nanny).* Joyce had rubbed elbows with her brother's famous friends before, and now she looked forward to some "red-carpet" gossip with me. But even with that catty conversation to look forward to, I had doubts.

What did a social worker like me have to say to the rich and famous? Just the thought of talking to them made me shaky. Privately, however, thinking of hobnobbing with the stars intrigued and excited me a bit. Wouldn't it be fun to escape single-mother work-work-work and come home with impressive stories that would boost my social status?

My boyfriend, not wanting to miss this "sure-to-be-fabulous" event, analyzed my reluctance as "just a little anxiety." All mixed feelings considered, it was an invitation I could not refuse.

Now I turned my attention to the top priority—the clothes! Bette from Boston was headed for Hollywood, and must be dressed "right." But exactly what was "right?" The memory of a past visit to Zeke's colored my perspective. We'd spent a "casual" evening at a restaurant popular with the Hollywood in-crowd. I was forewarned not to do what I most wanted to do—gawk! I was supposed to pretend that Rod and his wife were just like Joe and Marie next door? As I prepared for this latest star-studded adventure, I remembered that dinner.

Eight of us were seated at a round table in the middle of a well-appointed dining room. Despite the fact that "Perry Mason" had called to say he couldn't come, our table was satisfactorily interesting. The "table" was drinking expensive bottles of wine, and I was chatting to the man next to me, an actor from a popular TV series. From Curiosity Central I sneaked peeks at Pia and a couple other "names." Fortunately for me (and probably for them), Jack Lemmon and a few other unwatchables were dining in an adjoining room. But secretly and carefully I could assess the Hollywood dress code, uniquely L.A. expensive.

Then just as I was I regretting being dressed in my latest Boston bargain-basement treasure, the actor I was talking to dropped abruptly onto his plate. Now, remembering him passed out in his dinner was reassuring. If the party guests drank like this guy, no one would notice how I looked, and I could do a lot of gawking.

"But wait," I thought. "The women will look like those did. Yes, I need the right outfit!"

It was pricey, but I found it near my office in Back Bay. For several weeks I visited the outfit to (hopefully) catch a markdown. Wearing this, I would fit in. Finally I bought my ticket to Tinsel Town at fifty percent off. Two pieces of pure pink glamour—it was a stunner. A cowgirl-style shirt, bulging with shoulder pads, tapered to the waist, from where it flared softly over the gored, mid-calf A-line skirt. Bordered at shoulders and hips with triangular see-through plastic windows filled with opalescent sequins, the entire outfit sparkled with iridescent, multi-colored pink reflections.

Pink leather spike heels (I hate spikes, but this was special) and a dainty pink bag later, the finish was near. Only the jewelry selection remained. For this crucial choice I chose huge round silver earrings and a matching necklace covered with slivers of sparkling glass supposedly used on a shuttle mission. With sparkles and spangles shimmering pink, I was ready to go.

Set on a dry Hollywood hillside overlooking the lights of the San Fernando Valley, Zeke and Nina's house filled with people I wasn't supposed to ogle. The famous, soon-to-be, almost, and wannabes arrived as promised. Actors, directors, producers made entrances, including a short, vacant-looking man with a bright scarlet scarf who had acted in *Bonnie and Clyde*. Fran appeared with her trademark voice, and wound up in a corner next to a producer of art-house movies.

Party night was unusually warm and humid, and tables were set poolside. Large grills, firing up delicious aromas of juicy steaks and jumbo shrimp, promised an elegant dinner. Nina preferred the best, the biggest, and the most beautiful, but I was not intimidated. I was confident in my pink outfit, and delighted to be a part of what seemed like a movie scene. Relaxing now, I remembered something I had once learned about Nina, not expecting that this memory would shortly help me through an embarrassing—and, looking back, hilarious—situation.

During a previous visit Nina had proudly showed me her latest shopping-outlet bargain. This basic black sweater studded with gold beads was "marked down" to my monthly mortgage payment. But Nina was as thrilled with her "steal" as I would be with a $10 markdown. The part of me that wished I could look and be like Nina now understood that despite the difference in price and physical presentation, Nina was a lot like me.

When I first met her, I'd imagined Nina to be as self-assured inside as she was stunning outside. Much taller than I, and movie-star sexy, Nina turned heads. Yet on girlfriend afternoons she talked openly about her hurts and problems, happily skipping Rodeo Drive in favor of some big-box store. I loved being with Nina when she was just who she was. Despite the glamour and money differences, we both had our vulnerabilities and insecurities. But now it was party time, and Nina, beautifully poised and put together, was a charming and gracious hostess.

I wasn't doing too bad myself. During cocktails I had made it through introductions to several famous people without choking. One gentleman, a well-known director of theater in Boston, had compared me to some actress. Without referring to me by name (or looking at me!) he said to my date, "She looks like…"

"How rude!" I had thought with politically correct disdain. "The women are merely part of the scenery!" But to be honest, I did enjoy the sort-of attention, and silently patted myself on the back for the pink outfit. Now reasonably shed of insecurities and fortified with a little wine, I was ready for food.

Shortly after being seated outside, guests started filling plates with succulent mixed grill. Then within minutes thunder boomers began, bringing a sorely needed heavy downpour. Too vain to be drenched, grabbing plates and drinks, the hungry crowd crushed toward the only door into the house. The charge was on, and I did the only self-respecting thing I could do. I followed.

Suddenly I was wet. *The rain!* I thought, but I was wrong. Looking down, I saw that my cherished outfit was turning scarlet! In a torrent of horrified realization, it occurred to me that the rude director, again not seeing me, had bumped into me in the doorway with his latest glass of red wine.

Stained and mortified, I stood transfixed. Seeing my plight, Nina kindly insisted that her maid would know how to remove the spreading stain.

Too soiled and deflated to object, but still hopeful, I followed Nina and her maid to one of Nina's many humongous closets. There I limply handed over my outfit and surrendered to Nina's attempts to find a temporary replacement. Finally we settled on the only dress that *almost* fit.

Designed for a taller woman, the dress was at least one size too big and two seasons out of style. The sleeves flopped to my wrists, and the waist fell below my hips with a large sagging bow. I had hoped for something simple that would fit me, or one of Nina's sequined designer creations, but this thing she chose was a vividly hideous, screamingly gaudy, howling Halloween orange. Before the stroke of midnight, (or even 9 p.m.!) this Cinderella was turning into a pumpkin.

Maybe Nina's maid was a fairy godmother who would magically restore my dress. Alas, she was not, and the die had been cast. When dinner resumed in the house, Nina's maid presented both pink pieces in a plastic bag, soaked with club soda and tie-dyed a slimy sky-blue pink!

Overwhelmed and disappointed, I had a choice. I could face the stark naked reality of going back to the party feeling like a human orange in this oversized, hideous *thing,* or maybe I would just sulk in the comfort of this nether room until time to leave.

Damn! I thought, *after all my work to put that outfit together!* Nina had her tattooed eyelids and pouty mouth. Fran had her distinctive voice and walk, and the others all had their claims to fame. Without my outfit, what did I have to offer in this crowd?

As I contemplated my bad luck, a different thought surfaced into my awareness.

I remembered that under her beautiful exterior, Nina had shown me that she had a real Self, with real feelings and insecurities. Maybe these famous guests had their own issues under their fancy exteriors. Under pink or orange I, too had a real Self. In my non-Hollywood life, I taught stress management and helped people uncover their authenticity. Could I use my own strategies?

Could I accept the part of my Self that was disappointed and still draw from the confidence I am able to feel in other situations? Maybe I could stop being intimidated, stop comparing, and just be Me—a single mother, a strong, resilient woman, and the gawking tourist I had been warned not to be. I had handled crises worse than this. I did not have to let a fashion tragedy become a social or emotional disaster.

"I am as okay in orange," I reassured myself, "as I imagined I could only be in pink!" With these more uplifting thoughts, I returned to the party.

Staying centered in my wholeness, I adjusted my thinking, ate yummy food, focused on fun, had interesting conversations, and stared unselfconsciously to my heart's content. The beautiful house, alive with interesting people, provided a unique experience I most likely will never have again. With everyone eating and laughing, (and drinking!), only my bemused date and apologetic hostess even noticed that my color had changed. I, however, was acutely aware that my true colors were glowing, and I loved it!

I returned from Hollywood with a better story than I could have imagined. Once more I had seen the way in which the authentic Self is made up of colorful parts that include all sorts of mixed thoughts, feelings and beliefs, as well as the meanings we ascribe to past experiences. I had yet another reminder that when I know my Self, I have more choices. A part of me might always like to dress up, or make up, but when I need to cope, a strong part of me can show up.

As I discovered in Hollywood, a certain part of me was vulnerable to "shoulds." I had thought I should look a certain way to feel okay. At that fancy party, I discovered that wasn't true. But these realizations don't just switch on. They pulse, like a strobe light. First might come resentment or fear or some other painful emotion. Then it is as if a light goes on and for a second you feel ready to face the challenge. At times feelings can alternate quickly from minute to minute or sometimes day to day as you strive to cope. However, as time goes on you can find the insights to deal with your emotional stress and find what is true for your authentic Self.

Such was the case with Devorah, the courageous single mother who helped me launch this book. Devorah's unique circumstances might reflect experiences some of you have had.

When I first met her, Devorah had grown children. She was in contact with her 30-year-old daughter and estranged from her 20-something son. Devorah and I looked back on the circumstances of her single motherhood.

Devorah's is story of deep recovery, about a woman who did not avoid the pain she knew she would face as a single mother. Her story vibrates with her pain, her wisdom, and the courage of what she calls "the gift of desperation." Devorah took a path away from her first husband and ultimately even away from her children in order to reach her desired destination of wholeness.

DEVORAH'S STORY

"It is not any longer painful," Devorah told me. "I've come to an understanding of suffering and pain. There is pain. When you cut your finger, there is pain. Suffering is optional. You know, you can dress the cut and make yourself comfortable, but if you don't tend to it and you go around just saying 'see my wound,' then you are going to suffer. Looking back at the way I was, I can see that it's a lot easier to suffer than it is to grow. We can learn to tend the pain in a way that helps us to heal. Not just a Band-Aid®, but real healing. We will indeed hurt when there is a wound, but we can tend and grow, or we can suffer. The choice is ours."

When Devorah left her children's father, her husband of 17 years, she hoped the children would come with her and make a family unit. However, her two children chose to stay with their father, who had more financial resources than Devorah. They also had their father's extended family close by. Over the years Devorah tried to have the children stay with her, but she spent more time away from them than with them. With or without the kids, Devorah identified deeply with being a single mother, and believes her single mother journey led her to find her true Self.

About not having custody of her kids, Devorah told me, "While it was not my plan, both of my children, then 12 and 16, chose ultimately not to live with me. The strong part of me felt they were old enough to make that decision. I wanted them to be happy. I wanted them to have the house and their things, go to their schools, and keep in contact with their large family circle. I wanted their lives to be disrupted as little as possible by my decision. I knew that the household that I left them in was a better household than they would have had with me or if I had moved back with my parents. It's a fine line, but I knew they would be with people who cared about them."

Devorah went on to relate an earlier part of her story, a childhood littered with broken plates and a broken sense of Self. She talked about how she learned to hide who she was so she would never get blamed or shamed. After she lost touch with her children, she began to read books to find out about herself. Much of that understanding came when Devorah entered 12-Step recovery and began to grow in her program. "I began to see my own patterns and how I'd gotten where I'd gotten. During those years I came to know myself. I had a goal. When I did again meet with my children, I would be the most whole person I could be. The focus and love for my children was always there. My love for them was teaching me how to love myself."

Devorah talked to me about the need to differentiate from her children. Although she wasn't living with them her single motherhood still defined her, and her relationship with them was very much alive inside her. As Devorah spoke about the pain of not living with her children, she emphasized that she continued to feel that her own growth was analogous to theirs. As her journey continued and she learned more about her true Self, she came to realize that each one of them—mother, son and daughter—must indeed become his/her own person.

Devorah's story has wisdom about what goes on inside the heart and mind of the single mother, regardless of whether she lives with her children full-time, part-time or not at all. Her story relates the importance of accepting your own growth into wholeness while allowing the children to grow into Selves that are uniquely their own.

PUTTING PARTS TOGETHER:
SEVEN KEY BUILDING BLOCKS
OF THE SOLID SELF

While we might like to think that the true Self is composed only of the pink and pretty parts, the reality is that all people have many parts, all playing a part in who we truly are. Self parts emerge differently in different situations. The ability to recognize, identify and utilize the resources in various parts is called being "integrated." I refer to integration as "wholeness" or having a "solid" Self.

As you grow into greater wholeness and solid Self, you will be better able to understand what makes you tick. (Or what makes you sick.) With insight into your priorities, values and conflicts, you will have more power for decision-making and problem solving, and be better able to cope with the stresses of being a single mother.

Eliza, a 40-year-old single mother of two, explains "wholeness" as coming to recognize a mosaic of her whole Self that emerges even when she feels like she has broken into little fragments that make her feel scared and vulnerable.

I have identified seven key building blocks that will help you to be able to know the information and skills of your whole Self. While these blocks, like parts themselves, have differences based on age, experiences, family background, ethnicity, race, religion and various cultural values and expectations, they all have features that can assist you as you create a more solid Self. As you explore your story and understand yourself better, you can discover how to utilize these building blocks to stay solid when difficult issues arise.

THE SEVEN BUILDING BLOCKS OF SOLID SELF

1. Ability to recognize your parts and access their information and intuition for problem-solving.
2. Ability to think clearly and hold yourself together in difficult situations.
3. Ability to recognize the difference between what you can and cannot change.
4. Ability to be honest with your Self about yourself.
5. Ability to hold a no-blame, no-shame view of your life circumstances.
6. Ability to think clearly in order to accept your own choices and actions.
7. Ability to deal with painful emotions.

These characteristics make it possible for you to be with your Self and relate to others in more positive and effective ways.

As you go about life as a single mother, whether you realize it or not, what you say and what you do is influenced not only by parts of which you are conscious, but also by parts from which you are disconnected. However, you do not have to remain disconnected. You can make a conscious commitment to know what part is directing your actions. In doing so you will gain greater understanding of Self and tools to access the talents, strengths and insights in every part of you. The more you make friends with as many parts of your Self as you can, the more solid your core Self will become and the more whole and wise you will grow.

Bringing parts with which you have lost contact into consciousness and integrating them into your sense of who you are will take some time and effort, but it is possible. Some of your parts may surface spontaneously and you will naturally recognize them. Others may require professional assistance to uncover.

As I have grown through painful experiences of single motherhood, pursuing my own personal development, I have recovered and discovered exciting parts of myself such as my intuitive/spiritual/psychic part, and my passion for being a psychotherapist, a grandmother, and a writer. When you rediscover more of yourself, you can do more of what you need to do and you can benefit more from your experiences. You need all of you, or as much as you can muster at any given time, in order to heal, succeed, and become wise.

MY ROAD TO SOLID SELF

Many years before my Hollywood story, I would discover more about the solid Self, and about my true colors, through experiences far more difficult and painful than what happened at Zeke's party.

I grew up, married and divorced in three different socio-cultural decades. I wasn't a beatnik or a hippie, or caught up in the "free love" generation. I had done what I was told to do—marry, teach school, and raise kids. But conflicting messages of changing times affected me, starting poignantly at the end of high school.

At that time the parental message was "marry the *right* man." Translation: Jewish and well-off. Sadly, the young man I loved was neither. Attempts to convince my parents failed, and their pressure prevailed. I cut off the relationship, which left me stunted. I was no longer able to understand my preferences and choices—and feelings—in relationships. In addition, I was unable to recognize the grief I felt. As a result, the resources and emotions, important parts of my Self from which I had disconnected, would remain buried—alive—for many years.

Ironically, although it has taken years to understand, Dov was exactly the right man for me to marry. My marriage to Dov began a long journey on the road to find my solid Self. Eventually the pain of separation, divorce, and widowhood, as well as the struggles and the gifts of single motherhood and a deep commitment to Soul Mother Wisdom, would lead me back to my disconnected parts. But the road to solid Self takes some rocky turns, as it did for me several years and two kids into my marriage.

THE ROAD GETS ROCKY

Several years into our marriage Dov survived a major heart attack at age 30, and began reading books about open marriage. At the same time I was volunteering at a local counseling center. Dov was threatened by my interest in counseling, and I was threatened by his interest in extramarital relationships. As conflict and misunderstanding increased, the joy and connection I wanted from marriage disappeared.

When I discovered that Dov's interest in outside relationships was more than theory, my world was rocked. We tried to repair our marriage, but even with couples therapy it did not work. I still don't know if we lacked the know-how or just the commitment, but after a year or so Dov decided to leave the marriage. I was devastated, and my Self was in pieces. Panicked to my core, I truly thought I would fall apart.

At first I could barely function. A friend took care of my children while I sat immobilized. I didn't know who I was without the marriage that had given me identity. I longed for someone to tell me how to manage. But there were no blueprints, no how-to books, no computers and social networking. Living in a traditional married community, I knew few women in my situation. Dov had moved into a guesthouse, and I didn't know what role he would now play. I had two little girls who needed me more than ever, but I felt alone, unsure and insecure.

At that time I was most in touch with the part of me that wanted to run away and leave the enormous new responsibilities to someone else.

However, despite bone-numbing fear I wanted to be okay, and I desperately wanted my children to be okay. As I began to grasp the idea of "single" and "mother," my desire to get stronger got stronger. From this determined part more optimistic thoughts would occasionally break through, nourishing the thin roots of Self-confidence and courage that were beginning to grow.

Somewhat to my surprise and relief the scared part of me receded a bit, and the desire to overcome insecurities, to regain my sense of wholeness, to manage my life, and to feel good became as critical as the need to care for my children. With the help of some friends, a few colleagues at the counseling center, and my mother, I regained some balance. But I needed more.

I needed information, resiliency skills, and hope that I would be able to navigate this rocky road. I decided to stay open to what I could learn from my experiences, and from other people. Over the next few years I would find information and wisdom in often unpredictable and occasionally unwelcomed ways.

As I picked up my pieces, I would discover that maturity, resilience and strength were my true colors. Always tired, occasionally miserable, mostly determined, and oddly, a little excited, I committed myself to what would become the path to my solid Self and the road to Soul Mother Wisdom.

MY MOTHER'S COMFORT

Soon after Dov moved out, my mother moved in. Ironically my mother, whose messages about "the right" marriage had ultimately contributed to my predicament, would become my initial support. It was a relief to have another adult in the house. Mother cooked, shopped, did laundry and played with the kids, giving me respite from exhaustion and fear. At night she distracted me by beating me at Scrabble. While I complained about being left and losing, my mother soothed me with humor, describing the book we would write. The first chapter of our book was titled, "It's Enough Already!" In other words, "Your pain is too much for me to bear." Chapter Two was to be, "If This Keeps Up I'll Croak, You'll Croak and Then Where Will We Be?" In other words, "Get A Life!"

Though my mother must have hurt to see her daughter hurting, she did not join me in misery or dump any of her own painful feelings onto me. Apparently operating from a wise part of her Self, my mother offered empathy laced with as much stiff-upper-lip as we both could stand.

Ironically, the parent who told me that I would need a man to be okay was now helping me believe that I could be okay without one. Her implied message helped me find parts of my Self that I would need in this crisis and in others to come. My mother's belief in the courage I did not feel, and her unwavering support, gave me hope that I could survive. As I cried and we laughed, she helped me feel less victimized, allowing new strands of strength to germinate in my authentic Self. With my mother's comfort, I began to crawl slowly into healing.

KATY'S LESSONS

Despite my mother's reassuring presence, her comfort alone could not guide me through this new terrain of single motherhood. One part of me wanted to plead, "Mother, tell me *who I am?*" But my mother did not examine her own identity—how could I expect her to help me understand mine? After mother moved home, I continued searching for what I needed. Fortunately I knew Katy from our volunteer work at the local counseling center

Having brought up four children after her divorce, Katy knew a lot about being a single mother, and she understood my distress. For the next month Katy lived with me, tutoring me each evening with instructions on how to adjust my attitude from victim to victorious. Katy's lessons were serious, but delivered with compassion—and her own unique brand of humor.

Upon arrival, Katy presented me with a teeny wooden doll, a soldier with a certain anatomical part that stuck out when you pressed a button on the top of his head. Each time I crumpled into anger or tears Katy would hand the doll to me. I pressed, and our laughter created some healing space for my attempts to grasp Katy's lessons. With Katy's gentle, witty wisdom and our little wooden friend, I began to learn more about what it meant to have a solid Self, as a single mother and as a woman.

Following are Katy's lessons—and, parenthetically, some other thoughts from my less teachable parts.

- We all need support from other people, but your identity does not depend on a man or any other person. (But didn't I learn that my value as woman was based on the "right" husband—and his financial status?)
- You have strengths and abilities that you can learn to use. (Okay, that's nice—now let's finish this separation thing so I can rely on a "him" again.)
- You can—and will—survive on your own. (That sounds nice, but for someone else.)
- You can feel your feelings, and cope without wallowing in them. (Oh, come on, can't you see what he did to me?)
- You will grow more than you ever believed possible. (Great, but no thank you. Tell him to come back and save me from this mess!)
- Single Motherhood will have ups and downs, but *you will be okay.* (Duh?)
- You can survive without a man in residence. (No way!)
- You are capable, and someday will look back and be grateful for these experiences. (Is she kidding?)

Katy's wisdom highlighted the part of me that wanted to come to grips with reality and become stronger. Her lessons also sparked a desire to someday help other single mothers. Katy taught me the value of having support, and that being a single mother did not have to mean I was alone as a person. Although I still cried a lot and at times felt powerless, gradually I came to believe that I could be successful as a single mother. However, as I travelled this road I continued to learn more.

After Katy left, I turned to Brenda for support. Brenda offered advice of a different nature from Katy's lessons. Later, in other difficult times, what I learned from both of these single mothers would be helpful. But when I first spoke with Brenda, I was a bit puzzled, and in truth, a little put off.

BRENDA'S ADVICE

Brenda was one of the few single mothers I knew. Divorced and raising three kids, she appeared to enjoy single motherhood. Brenda also had a bravado that made me wonder what she could offer.

"You can do whatever you *want* now, Brenda fiercely advised. "You don't have to ask *him* if it's ok. They are *all yours* now."

All mine?

That didn't interest me one bit, and I couldn't fathom Brenda's delight. Didn't kids need their dads too, when possible? Was Brenda saying that she didn't co-parent with her former husband? Although I had no formal training at the time, I sensed that parental cooperation was best for kids. I also sensed an underlying angry edge to Brenda's comments. However, at the time I didn't know how to ask the questions that might have lead to an explanation.

In her own way Brenda's advice helped me integrate a piece of Soul Wisdom into my true Self. Although Brenda's rather militant way seemed to work for her, and maybe for her children, it was not for me. However, Brenda helped me decide to consciously co-parent with Dov and to keep the girls connected to him and to his family. Ironically, as it turned out, Brenda's best advice was unintentional. She taught me that there is a big difference between coming on strong and *being* strong.

What I learned from my mother, Katy, and Brenda helped me in different ways. By then Dov had moved to the next town, and I was set to be a single mother for better or for worse. Thanks to my divorce settlement, I was also set to begin social work school. Poised on these two tracks, I was feeling reasonably settled and proceeding as courageously as I could into my new life. However, three years later my ability to hold my Self and my world together would again be challenged.

THE ROAD GETS ROCKIER

After social work school graduation, I took a low-pay, high-satisfaction job at the local Jewish Community Center. I also began a small private practice in Boston with two male friends. I didn't have money, but I had hope. Then one late August night when my girls were 9 and 12, my fragile security, and our stability, were shaken by a crisis that would require every available part of my Self to cope.

On a hot, quiet Friday afternoon, Dov arrived to pick up the girls to spend the weekend with him and his wife and new baby. However, I had already driven the girls to his house. For a brief moment we were alone on the porch. Standing there, we silently faced each other. Dov was wearing a white shirt and looked handsome. I was aware that my old resentful part was being replaced by unexpected affection.

"They're at your house," I said. "I'm sorry you had to come for nothing."

"It's okay," he replied emphatically, looking at me with kind eyes. "It's all okay."

Those were Dov's last words to me.

Within hours the man I had loved, hated, fought with, divorced and sometimes missed, the man who'd fathered my children, was dead. He suffered a fatal heart attack in the night.

Trying to grasp the reality paralyzed me with emotions so intense that I couldn't eat, sleep, or move. For days my cousin and my mother cared for the children while I sat and stared. Although now more than ever did I need a wise inner core, my Self was shaken to its root. My only thoughts were questions and more questions.

Is this real? How can I help my girls through their loss when I cannot fathom my own? Will I function again? What about money? Where will my place be in my former family now that there's a widow and a baby boy? And what about this feeling of love? Was I a widow too? I felt like one. Dov had been a decently involved single dad. How could I raise the kids completely on my own? How can we be okay without him? Most of these questions could only be answered over time, but in the meantime mourning brought up the full range of feelings.

Like emotional strobe lights, my feelings pulsed between sadness, anger, fear and almost unbearable grief. At times I even felt relief. Oddly, it occurred to me that in some way single mothering might be easier. Surprisingly, grappling with my new reality brought me back to Brenda's advice. Her words, once confusing, now offered a strange comfort.

Yes, they were *"all mine"* now, and a part of me I had not recognized before felt a sense of possessiveness. Now I would make all the decisions. No longer did I have to consult with the other parent regarding schedules and sharing. And I would be spared the feelings of loss or competition as I watched the girls leave for fun with their father.

I began to have a little glimpse of what Brenda had been trying to tell me, but I wouldn't know for many years that my possessive part, too, would have to be dealt with. Later, when new people would come into the girls' lives, Soul Mother Wisdom would have other guidance and other lessons about letting go.

However, despite new insight into Brenda's style, it was still not mine. The new meaning of "All Mine" terrified me, and I couldn't imagine a world without my children's father, or my next version of "Being Okay."

THE ROAD TO WISDOM

Despite the many challenges I faced and the ongoing fear I felt, I refrained from using my girls as supports. As I began to put life's pieces back together, I sought out peers for emotional support. I tuned in to my inner guidance as much as possible, and in the midst of the emotional quicksand threatening to suck me down, inner wisdom helped to pull me up.

"I survived separation and divorce!" I said to myself. "I have a good support network and marketable skills. With hard work, the girls and I can be okay." Strengthened by this type of thinking, I continued on a road that began before Dov and I divorced. Early on we had explored the healing power of the mind. I had learned that what you focus on can affect how you feel. Later, scientific research would confirm this as bio-neurologically accurate, but at the time I was more interested in emotional survival, and wisely, I began concentrating on *feeling* strong.

Now I took steps to affirm that I could cope, and that my girls and I would be okay. When I felt afraid, I meditated on confidence. When I felt anxious, I increased conscious contact with inner guidance. One way I did this was to imagine a creatively stocked healing room that I could visit during meditation. Using this imagery I was able to reduce negative thinking, lower my stress, and increase energy for problem solving and enjoyment of life. You might like to create your own healing room. You can recreate your room or create additional rooms whenever you wish. Feel free to give it a try.

YOUR OWN HEALING ROOM

Begin with an easy breath, feeling your shoulders relax as you breathe gently in and out. Now, breathing normally, imagine entering a place that has special significance for you. It might be a place you have been, or a place that you create in your imagination.

Use your senses to see, feel, taste, smell and hear the unique features of your special room as you design its magical and mystical healing powers perfectly suited to your personal needs and wants.

You can picture healing equipment, magic potions and mystical advisors who can provide you with the peace and comfort needed for any strength you would like to develop. You can change the features of your room anytime you wish, and create other rooms that serve healing purposes.

If you wish you can bring imaginary counselors into your room. Use your full creative imagination. Your counselors can be people, animals, or plants, living or departed. You can have special rocks and crystals. You can create special sounds and videos that will give you the insights for strength, courage, resilience, or any other qualities you seek.

Now you can spend a few moments in this healing space, affirming that time spent here can promote restoration of your energy and offer soul guidance for your problems. As you relax peacefully, just notice what thoughts and ideas enter your mind. You may have memories or emotions arise. You can allow them to come in and go out as you breathe. Affirm that negative thoughts will have no ill effect on you.

Before reorienting to your environment, affirm that you can return, relaxed and restored. Affirm that you will be impressed with guidance right away, or later. Affirm that each time you enter your special space you will receive healing benefits that will bring your special brand of well-being to your body, mind and spirit.

GUMMY'S INSPIRATION

With these efforts to restructure my life and provide for my little family, fear faded a bit. Contact with Soul Mother Wisdom increased, as did my trust that we would be okay. I found new venues for teaching stress management, and a small regular check from Dov's estate helped.

My two partners and I built up our Boston practice, and I continued part time at the community center, where the girls could be with me for activities after school. I paid a neighbor to assist the children with homework and meals when I was in the city.

These complex arrangements worked for a while, but as the girls' needs increased, so did the need for money. The time had come to leave my job at the center, which, despite low pay, offered community and comfort. Facing the challenge of creating full-time private practice was scary, and meant another major change. I put off the decision until a dream about my grandmother inspired me to know what was right for me to do.

Gummy had a beautiful but untrained singing voice. When she was young, a talent agent had requested permission to put Gummy on the stage. But my great-grandfather said no, decreeing that vaudeville was no place for a respectable young lady. Every time Gummy told this part of her story, I could hear her disappointment. But in my dream, I heard only her beautiful voice and her Soul-inspired wisdom.

In an iridescent bubble of glowing light, Gummy hovered above me. She appeared young and beautiful, and her face radiated love. And Gummy was singing. When her sweet song ended, Gummy spoke softly, and her message was clear.

"My child," Gummy said, "They wouldn't let me sing. But you can do what you want, and need, to do. Do not let anyone or anything hold you back. *You will be okay.*"

Gummy's wisdom rang true in my Soul, and I resigned the next day.

As Gummy promised, I was okay, and we were okay. With a lot of focused effort I started a second practice in my house, and continued in Boston. Although I was exhausted most of the time from doing it all, we managed and I felt grateful. The children, and the work, were "all mine," and I was keeping myself together. But a few years into this new arrangement another crisis threatened our stability, making me once again wonder if we would be okay.

I AM ROCKETED INTO ACTION

I now had two money-making therapy practices, and the girls were okay, doing the typical things that kids do. I was in therapy, learning about emotions long buried and how courageous parts of my solid Self were helping me survive. Dov's father was generously paying our heating bills, but a problem was brewing underneath my tentative emotional security and my fragile financial stability that once more rocked my life.

Although Dov's widow had inherited his half of our house, I paid the mortgage, and her ownership had not been a problem. Then one day my former father-in-law came to visit bringing shocking news. What he had to say would lead me to find a part of my Self that was willing to fight to the finish to protect what was going to be "all mine."

The small amount of money from Dov's estate that I received for the girls, their grandfather said, was almost gone. Having had no warning, I was stunned. Evidently Dov had died with an insurance policy that "would have taken care of everyone" sitting on his desk, unsigned. This was bad enough, but what my former father-in-law said next almost knocked me over.

This fatherly man, in many ways a caretaker, who had stayed close to his grandchildren, spending time with them and kindly paying for their orthodontia, matter-of-factly spelled out our fate. Dov's widow now needed money. If I wanted to keep the house, I was to buy out her half in cash—only cash, and a lot of cash. No, she would not take a personal mortgage, and no, he was not offering financial help.

Their lawyers and accountants had figured the value of her half, and their figure was nonnegotiable. Although I had received a lump sum of money for the girls' college after Dov died, it was not enough. Besides, I'd had to use a lot of it to take care of the house and the girls as I was building my career. Not only did I not have the amount of cash she demanded, but I did not make enough to qualify for a mortgage. In that case, my former father-in-law suggested, I could sell my house and move into an apartment in a more "affordable" community.

As much as he loved my children, their grandfather was obviously oblivious to the huge impact such a change could have on them. I was horrified. My girls had been through a divorce and the death of their father, and I was determined that they have no more loss. Somehow—I had no idea how—I would do what I had to do to keep us in our home. But part of me felt beaten, and longed for someone to save me. At first I just sat in fear and disbelief and cried. So much work, and now we could lose so much.

Although I knew I needed all of me to overcome this latest disaster, at first there was little of me available. Once again I had to figure out how to go on. (Or maybe cry on the couch forever, and let life go on without me!) But eventually, cried out, exhausted, frightened, enraged, and in a blur, I got up. While sitting with and accepting my thoughts and feelings, I found the courage to stand up to the challenge. Pouring out my emotions had helped me feel and face my sadness and fear. These feelings were real parts of me, and I had learned what could happen when emotions get cut off.

A resilient part knew how to cope with adversity. An intuitive part would lead me through the dark. I would rocket into action and fight for our house, for our safety, and for the way of life my children knew. Gummy had said I would be okay. I would again prove her right. I would trust that the wisdom that had guided me in previous crises would see me through this one.

For weeks I lived under the pressure of coming up with the cash. To make matters more complicated, my older daughter was getting ready for college, which also meant money. I cried many more times, and as many times reminded myself of Gummy's prediction. Although at times I felt overwhelmed with fear, I stayed connected to the part of me that believed in my Self. I reaffirmed my willingness, and ability, to do the hard work. I focused on having the confidence to succeed. And I discovered a part of me that was stronger than I ever dreamed.

With my lawyer's help I took a loan on the college money. I gave my diamond ring to mother to sell. "It didn't work anyway," I told her. And I used a tiny inheritance received from a recently deceased relative. I did other things I no longer remember, and finally I had the cash in hand and handed it over. I had done what I needed to do. But I had not done what I needed *not* to do.

I did not tell my children about this crisis. Oh, part of me would have loved to vent to my kids. But inner wisdom said *"Don't!"* and I listened. I needed to *not* dump my feelings onto my children. They had lived through enough tough realities, and they could be confused by hearing my negativity. Despite my distress I wanted to spare their tender psyches contamination by my anger, fear and disappointment, and ensure the uncomplicated relationships with Dov's family that my girls deserved.

But I am no saint, and was no stranger to feelings of resentment or victim thinking. I screamed and cried plenty in rage and outrage, but not to my kids. I vented instead to friends. And although I could not see it then, the time would come much later when I would understand that neither my former father-in-law or Dov's widow intended harm. Despite the fact that they were willing to put my children's home on the chopping block, they were hurting too, and doing the best they could.

I *think* I know (and like to believe) that my choices have contributed to the wonderful adults my daughters have become, and that the loving relationships they have maintained with their father's family, especially with their half-brother, have enriched their lives. However, I positively do know that each time inner wisdom has guided my thinking and my choices, I have been given opportunities to develop the inner strength that can come from dealing with adversity, as well as the wisdom and peace of mind that can come with acceptance. And I have been okay.

TIPS FOR UNDERSTANDING

Please bear in mind that healing goes at its own pace. Sometimes one incident can give you a leap, and other times a little boost. Whether at this moment you are healing slowly or quickly, the following tips can help you access inner wisdom and take effective action. As you face your enormous responsibilities, with these tips, you will be better equipped to stay solid in tough situations, using the resources in your parts, and growing more competent and confident as a single mother.

As you become more solid, and develop your authentic sense of being whole, you can come to trust that you can handle whatever comes your way, and that you and your children *can* be okay.

Five Tips for Staying Solid, Using Wisdom, and Being Okay

Tip One: Notice What You Think and Feel and Do

Noticing what you think and feel, and observing what you do, can teach you a lot about the parts of your Self. You will recognize and identify with some parts easily, while others containing mixed emotions and thoughts may be harder to accept. While it might be easier to identify with parts of your Self that hold positive emotions such as happiness, satisfaction and joy, parts that contain more painful emotions, such as anger, fear, or grief, are also part of your wholeness.

One way to increase awareness of your various feelings and thoughts, or to review your actions, might be to use the "pages for journaling" at the end of each chapter to jot notes about what you notice. The more you know about your whole Self, the more solid you can become. At times professional assistance may be useful to help you understand the parts of your Self more fully.

Tip Two: Accept Your Wholeness

Go easy on yourself when you notice less "pretty" parts. There is no need to feel ashamed or guilty for having negative thoughts or painful emotions. Use a no-blame, no-shame perspective as you recognize and observe the parts of your authentic Self. Both positive as well as negative feelings are normal. Consider this: the negative and painful parts of your Self have a positive side, for they show you where you can grow and where you need to heal.

The more you come to know, acknowledge, and accept the parts of your whole Self, the more wise you will grow, the more conscious your decisions will be, and the more effective your actions will become. You will feel more in charge of your life, with fewer instances of asking yourself "Why did I say or do *that?*" You can better understand the motivations of your choices and actions because they will be based on your awareness of your authentic Self. You will better understand the intentions and motivations of your choices because they will be based on awareness of your authentic Self.

Tip Three: Tune into Your Wise Inner Voice

With awareness and acceptance of your parts, you can more effectively and easily interpret wisdom from your inner voice. However, to interpret inner wisdom accurately, it is necessary to be able to differentiate your mind from someone else's. Refraining from assuming you know what another person is thinking, or what you think they think you should do, can make you more open to your own wisdom.

When a "should" from someone else comes into your mind, check with your Self to see if this resonates with what's right for you. If it's your own "should" that comes up, you can practice changing it to a "want" and see how that "want" resonates with your truth. This technique can help you be more in tune what your true wisdom is advising.

Tip Four: Increase Wisdom by Changing Your Perspective

Wisdom from positive parts of your wholeness can play an important role in helping you change your perspective on your problems. Single moms typically have a number of problems that are disturbing, infuriating, and/or beyond their control. However, just as disturbing may be the mistaken belief that you can change or control what you cannot. Differentiating what is in your control and what is not constitutes a strong coping tool, and a crucial piece of Soul Mother Wisdom.

The Serenity Prayer contains powerful wisdom for single moms. "God grant me the serenity to accept the things I cannot change, the courage to change the things I can, and the wisdom to know the difference."

Even when you can't control or change circumstances, you *can* change the way you think about them. When you have "the wisdom to know the difference" you will be better equipped to stay solid and know what action is called for in a particular situation. When you reroute your attitude, you may be delighted to find that you feel more empowered, more peaceful, and more solid.

Tip Five: Meet Your Emotional Needs

When you're distressed, it's natural to want to grumble to those closest to you. It would be easy to use your children as your supports and consultants. However, even in the most upsetting situations, it's in the kids' best interest to just be the kids, and for you to find appropriate adult support.

By staying aware of what you and the kids need—and what the kids do *not* need, such as your anxiety and fears dumped on them—you will be better able to make decisions that are in the best interests of you and of them in both the short and long term.

Most of us have erred by complaining or venting to the kids about how upset (afraid, angry, frustrated, victimized, hurt, etc.) we are. If you slip up (and you will!), just correct course. You can apologize to the kids, but that's not always necessary. You can forgive yourself and pledge to find the correct outlets going forward. Kids are resilient, and single mothers are, too. You can override slip-ups with your wisdom and strength, and you can trust that the kids and you can be okay!

IDEAS FOR REFLECTION AND INSIGHT

It takes a great deal of courage to pursue and to keep a vision of life that is bright and satisfying, rather than miserable and draining. At various times you may experience life at either extreme with emotional variations in between. While mothering as a single parent may sometimes feel like something you just have to endure, at other times you might choose to see your life as an adventure that can lead to hidden treasures.

While it's true that when you must stay home from work with a sick child and still have enough to pay the rent a positive view of things is hard to maintain, I offer you this idea: having a solid sense of Self and a balanced vision of your life can help you weave through your experiences, and lead to your becoming a more effective mother and a stronger individual.

At any given moment the choice of how to view your life is your own. As you reflect on your story, bear in mind that when it comes to emotional pain, there's a paradox; pain can be the gift that gets you going, and forces you to grow. While some emotions hurt and can distract or derail you, the more painful ones offer opportunity. As you recognize and understand what you're feeling, you can learn to locate the center of resilience and strength from which you can make effective choices and live an enlightened life.

In difficult, embarrassing, or painful circumstances you can learn to call upon the wise and intelligent parts of your Self. Your parts, more and more integrated into solid wholeness, will direct you to clear thinking and correct action. Your solid inner core can help you decrease anxiety, heal negative emotions, and build mastery over your single-mother life.

You might want to take some time now to reflect, and use the journaling pages to jot down a few thoughts about your personal road to wholeness. In doing so, you may be pleased to see how your parts fit into the whole picture of your authentic Self. As you reflect, you might consider these questions:

What parts of your Self do your recognize?
If you drew a picture of yourself, what colors would you use for your parts?
What events have helped particular parts to evolve?
If you had a conversation with your Self portrait, what wisdom does each part offer?
What Self parts have helped you with a certain problem?
What did this experience teach you about your solid Self?
What people have been your teachers?
What advice has helped and what advice has been important to let go?
What strength has kept you from passing negative emotions to your kids?
When your road gets rocky, how will you remember to use the strengths in your parts?

If you find yourself wondering how you handled something that you thought you couldn't, or if you find yourself saying something like "Wow, that is not like me to say or do that"—whether you think the action was positive or negative—you may be close to discovering an unrecognized part of yourself that you can integrate into your Whole Authentic Self.

PAGES FOR JOURNALING

This might be a good moment to write down some feelings, thoughts, and experiences that have led you to recognize the parts of your solid Self.

There is no right or wrong in journaling. Just allow the thoughts, memories, and feelings to arise.

Of course, you can come back to these pages any time you wish. Trust that wise knowing is always available whenever you quiet your mind and listen to your inner "voice."

As you open your mind to the Soul Wisdom within, the more you will come to know your true Self, the more empowered you will be, and the more you will discover that you and your children can be okay.

INSIGHT THREE

Soul Mother Wisdom Empowers
Your True MRS

"I used to confuse my sadness with my Self. Feelings must be faced and worked through. They are part of the true Self. Authentic wholeness can become a love story with your Self."

SINGLE MOTHER, CIRCA 2007

I TRADE MRS. FOR MRS

Before deciding to proceed with divorce, I had a surprising experience of soul wisdom that showed me a Self more solid and more whole than I could have imagined.

One evening Dov surprised me by saying that he wanted to get back together. There'd been a time I'd hoped to hear that, but now I felt confused and tempted.

I remembered the intense sadness I'd felt when we separated, and I flashed on the reality of the mega responsibility (and minor alimony and child support) of my new life. What a relief to be a Mrs. again! If I said "No, thank you!" life would continue with huge demands and difficult emotions. A scared part of me pulled toward the fantasy of safety and wanted to shout, "Let's go for it!"

Then, almost instantly, *knowing* emerged from a different part of my Self. Not in pictures and not in words, but in a moment of intuitive insight the "voice" of my authentic Self, of my soul, *told* me, and showed me, the correct choice. There had been troubling issues between Dov and me, none of which had been resolved during our separation. I saw that back together there would be new and different stressors, possibly more challenging, than those I now had. I understood that with "Yes!" an essential opportunity for further development of wholeness and wisdom would be gone.

In this moment of true Self, I *knew* that the strong core of my inner spirit would guide the continuation of my journey to maturity, resilience, and strength. And I *knew* this was the right choice for me.

Soul Wisdom was allowing me to see that as hard as it was, and as hard as it might become, the children and I would be okay. For becoming a stronger woman and a more competent mother, I *needed* my single mother life!

But wait! Dov was saying that he would marry someone else if I said "No." The door to reunion of our two-parent family would close. His new wife would take my place in the extended family I loved, and I would have to cope with another bout of sadness from that already painful loss. In addition to grappling with grief, I would need to work hard to keep the children's lives and our financial situation stable.

Although I sensed that difficulties lay ahead, the guidance was clear, and I chose to listen. Disappointed and angry, Dov went his way. And, stunned by my courage, I went mine. Amazingly—or maybe not— the following years provided the opportunities, and the hardships, that Soul Mother Wisdom had so accurately foreseen.

Dov did marry someone else. And with peer and professional help I was able to progress into healing. I dealt with my feelings and my losses, and experimented with new relationships. Thanks to the time Dov spent with the girls, as well as to my own creative time management, I finished social work school, began my clinical career, cultivated a wider personal support network, and found enough Self-strength and Soul Wisdom to juggle it all with parenting skills I didn't even think I had!

Although I could not have known that Dov would die so young, when that tragedy occurred I was managing single mother life and engaged in a journey to wholeness that I had sensed, but could not, even in an epiphany, fully envision. I have gratefulness for having been given a chance to "practice" the skills and strengths I would need when I would become my children's only living parent. Could it have been that Soul Mother Wisdom knew I needed preparation for the enormous stressors and responsibilities of an even more difficult era of my single mother life?

Of course, I have often wondered how things might have turned out had I said, "Yes." But I have never doubted the rightness of my choice. In fact, I have come to more deeply understand the necessity to follow Soul Mother Wisdom. I believe that at that point in my life, for the empowerment of wholeness and wisdom I needed to relinquish being a "Mrs." for the sake of my "true MRS."

Once I'd believed that a "Mrs." in front of my name gave me identity and made me whole. However, I've learned that *true* wholeness of solid Self is made up of your parts, their qualities, and their resources. Your wholeness helps you make effective choices and holds you together "in one peace" when the going gets rough.

As one single mother told me, "Whether you chose your single mother state or it was chosen for you, you need time to discover your Self. Now it's about the journey, not about the destination."

TRUE MRS

While there are a variety of positive qualities to your wholeness of Self, there are three I consider to be crucial. I call these key qualities *Meta-maturity, Responsive-resilience,* and *Self-strength,* and refer to them simply as "true MRS." Your wholeness and soul wisdom empowers the development of these three key qualities, while in return your true MRS inspires your wisdom and builds your solid central core of Self.

Meta-maturity is the developed way of thinking about your Self and your choices that allows you to achieve personal healing, realize single mother success, and access Soul Mother Wisdom. With Meta-maturity you are able to work through painful emotions and use inner knowing to inform effective parenting and guide life decisions. Meta-maturity allows you to evaluate the consequences of your actions and replace unproductive coping strategies as needed.

Responsive-resilience is the cultivated ability to use clear thinking, effective strategies, and inner wisdom to respond successfully to parenting problems, single-mother dilemmas, and the general demands of life. With Responsive-resilience you are able to understand the influence of your thoughts and emotions on your actions, and you know how to address your children's needs without sacrificing your own. Responsive-resilience empowers the courage, energy, and know-how to rebound from adversity and continue to make life fulfilling.

Self-strength is the practiced ability to manage stress, deal with painful emotions, and use effective coping skills to hold your Self together, even when you feel like you're falling apart. Self-strength is derived from using Soul Mother Wisdom along with non-distorted thinking when solving difficult problems and making life decisions. Self-strength fortifies you by keeping you connected to the inner wise guidance of your authentic Self.

Please bear in mind that these three crucial qualities overlap and depict the ideal. No single mother—no one—can be perfect. However, as you cultivate these qualities, your true MRS can become the foundation on which you can heal from disappointments and losses and build a satisfying life as a single mother, and as a woman.

True MRS enables you to:

- Base your identity on your intrinsic worth, rather than on others' opinions and outside influences.
- Think clearly, manage your emotions, and gain insight into your authentic Self.
- View circumstances, life changes and adversity as opportunities for growth.
- Use inner wisdom, stress management skills, and common sense to adapt to circumstances and cope with problems.
- Replace fear, doubt, insecurity and victim thinking with the knowledge that you are a competent woman doing the best you can, and that your best is good enough.
- Be flexible enough, and sensible enough, to know when you require outside support, and be willing to seek it.
- Hold others realistically accountable, and practice forgiveness to benefit your own peace of mind.
- Take responsibility for your own choices with a no-blame/no-shame attitude, while staying open to learning from both welcomed and unwelcomed consequences of your actions.
- Know what you can control and what you cannot, because understanding the difference leads to Soul Wisdom.

- Trust the wisdom of your parenting strategies and choices, and evaluate the outcomes realistically. Correct course as needed without putting yourself down.
- Put your children first without putting your Self last.
- Stay in one Peace when playing the hand you've been dealt makes you feel like you're going to pieces.

With true MRS you will have more know-how for dealing with your life and your feelings. Neither hard times nor other people's opinions will be able to rob you of your wisdom.

As you mature, your coping choices will be based on awareness of your motivations and intentions. With resilience you will be able to use careful reasoning along with intuition for parenting and living. Self-strength will give you the confidence to know what to do, even when you don't know what you're doing!

The journey to true MRS can take you through some difficult terrain. However, the attitudes and skills of Meta-maturity, Responsive-resilience and Self-strength will increase your coping power, strengthen the wholeness of your solid Self, force you to grow in Soul Mother Wisdom, and move you toward mastery of the seven critical tasks.

SEEKING THE SOLID CENTER OF SELF: A JOURNEY

In her book *Desperately Seeking Self: An Inner Guidebook for People with Eating Problems,* Viola Fodor offers a message that eloquently describes the core essence of the solid center of Self.

> You have within you an essence, a core, your essential self. It goes deeper than all of your limiting, negative self-identities....When you experience self, you will know it. Every situation, every aspect of your life will be suffused with awareness, beauty, compassion, goodness, wisdom and strength. It is only when you are not connected to your inner self that life can seem shallow and pointless, even desperately out of control.

Some people like to describe journeys of Self development as linear progressions, with distinct starting points followed by stages to be mastered as you move forward. In a linear view, depending on circumstances, you may go back to a previous stage to continue your growth. While linear views have much insight to offer, envisioning your single-mother journey as a circle offers a unique way of understanding the process by which you develop a solid core of authentic Self and develop Meta-maturity, Responsive-resilience, and Self-strength, your true MRS.

Although I am far from an expert in physics, I use the centripetal force requirement as a metaphor to help explain the way in which single mother life moves you toward the solid center of your authentic Self. The centripetal force requirement explains that objects moving in a circular motion exert a force that causes the objects to seek the center.

In a circular concept of Self development, the centripetal force requirement makes "soul" sense as well as physical sense. Viewing the growth of your authentic Self, your true MRS, as a circular dynamic suggests that life events exert a centripetal force that continually moves you to a destination of MRS, authentic wholeness, and your central core of Soul Mother Wisdom.

A circular view of development can also be reassuring, for rather than thinking that you're slipping backwards when the road gets rough, you can remind yourself that you're on a path in which every point becomes a destination of strength. With this understanding you can feel more empowered and experience a greater sense of confidence as you deal with life. You can realize that achieving Meta-maturity, Responsive-resilience, and Self-strength is never a finished product, but merely a natural cycle of healing, succeeding, and becoming wise as you continue to seek the wisdom at the center of your solid Self.

I have identified three critical points, or key positions, along the journey to the center of Self and true MRS. The three points are the **Position of Forming Positive Self-Identity,** the **Position of Achieving Effective Adaptation,** and the **Position of Generating Restorative Stability.** As each position on the circle blends into the next, you will encounter challenges unique to your particular point in the cycle. Each time you manage and master a challenge with Soul Mother Wisdom, you will generate positive energy that will bring you closer to the central core of your true Self.

To deal with the challenges that arise when moving toward, or spending time in, a key position, you can use a variety of coping strategies and tips. Many are mentioned in this chapter, and you will find useful strategies throughout this book. Often overlapping, but applicable in any position, the strategies can help cultivate the attitudes and skills you need for becoming a wiser single mother, and a more fulfilled human being.

FORMING POSITIVE SELF-IDENTITY

Forming a positive Self-identity as a worthy and competent person is a fundamental building block of authentic Self for everyone. For single mothers, there is an additional and crucial element for the development of positive Self-identity. Single mothers must reject three mistaken stereotypes: 1) That one-parent households are broken; 2) That single moms raise bad kids; and 3) That you did something wrong to become a single mother in the first place.

For your positive Self-identity to grow as a single mother, you may need to answer questions like these:

Who am I? Who is my family?

Does what I'm doing with my life matter?

How am I going to raise my kids to be strong and healthy, do everything I have to do, and feel good about myself while I do it all?

Your answers can include these affirmations:

I am doing one of the most important jobs on the planet.

I matter as person and as a mother.

On my journey to wholeness I can have a good life.

I believe that my family is whole—because it is—and so am I.

Being a single mother does not mean there's something wrong with you. Your children can grow up strong and healthy and you can take care of yourself, too! You don't have to be perfect to be effective.

My own entry into single motherhood presents a good example of the "who am I" challenge for forming a positive identity.

As a two-parent family, we often skied together. When Dov and I first separated and the girls went skiing with their father, I felt like an amputated limb. At times I hurt so bad that my mental attitude dissolved into lies about my worth. It was as if I was no longer connected to "me." Fortunately, one day I brought my false Self perceptions to my therapist. "I will never ski again!" I told Joleen, with an emphasis on "never." Joleen wisely challenged my distorted beliefs about myself.

"Bette," she gently admonished, "no other person is your arms and your legs! If you want to go skiing, take your daughters skiing!"

For a moment I was taken aback. Go without my husband? This had never occurred to me. But Joleen's words made me think. Maybe I could do it. We already had the equipment, I had what passed for a car, and of course (important insight!) I still had my limbs. But I didn't have much money. Maybe with some budget creativity, I could scrape together enough for a day trip to a close mountain—

With this glimpse of a new possibility, I got some friends together for a day trip to some nearby slopes. There, while on a run with the girls, a perception shifted. I was doing this on my own! With the right support, could I do other things with the kids?

This moment of energized Soul Mother Wisdom helped me feel whole as a single mother, and forced me closer to my central core of MRS.

Most single mothers with whom I have spoken relate having experienced similar shifts in awareness. After being thrown (or having jumped) head first into one of the biggest identity crises of life, most single mothers need some time, some encouragement, and some support to realize that we are not broken. We must come to affirm that we can still function, that we are still whole, that we can be good mothers, and that we can even have fun.

STRATEGIES AND TIPS FOR FORMING POSITIVE SELF-IDENTITY

It is essential that you cultivate trust in your basic worth, because single motherhood can pack a proverbial wallop. Good or bad, circumstances do not define you, but the way you respond to them can help you to grow. Keeping an open channel to soul wisdom can help you stay positive about your Self, and can help you keep in mind the following tips and strategies:

- Refute stereotypes that single mothers and their families are "broken."
- Believe that you are a whole person with or without a partner.
- Cultivate an optimistic view of yourself and your family, and consciously return to it when it slips away.
- Trust that you do not need to be a perfect single mother to be a successful single mother.
- Tune to the guidance of Soul Mother Wisdom for parenting and living.
- Know your thoughts and work through your emotions for better understanding of your solid Self.
- Learn how to neutralize negative Self talk by creating positive Self suggestions and affirmations.

Remember to do whatever gives you respite from your daily juggling act. You can meditate, but it can be just as effective to sit in your favorite chair, listen to music, read a good book, or relax in a tubby. Take a short walk or watch your baby sleep. These moments of *be-ing* with yourself can connect you to wisdom and help integrate your parts into the positive central core of your Self-identity. During these times you can use affirmations to keep your mind-set positive, improve your ability to manage life, and ratchet up your maturity, resilience, and strength.

The following affirmation might be helpful now, or later. Taking a gentle breath, feel yourself ease into a peaceful state of mind, and read or say:

As I connect to the wisdom inside, I am guided to correct thinking and action. Maturity, resilience, and strength form the foundation of my Self. Every day, in every way, I am growing into wholeness of Self. My children and I constitute an intact family in which we all can thrive. Negative thoughts have no ill effect on me. I am able to take care of my children and myself. I have the mental and emotional capacity to cope. I will know how to find the supports I need one day at a time. I am able to stay in one "peace" even when I feel like I am going to pieces.

As I continued to move forward toward the center of positive Self-identity, I gained more confidence in my ability to make a good life. There were more times when it occurred to me that I could be okay as a single mother. Given more comfort in my single motherhood, and in my Self, I was moving into the next Position, of Effective Adaptation.

ACHIEVING EFFECTIVE ADAPTATION

The ability to rebound from difficult situations requires resilience, and constitutes a major challenge in achieving effective adaptation. A positive Self-identity can help you come to grips with what single-mother life deals out. Stress management strategies, which will be discussed in detail in Chapter Four, can foster your Self-awareness and help you make the best parenting and life decisions possible. In the Position of Achieving Effective Adaptation, Responsive-resilience will increase, enabling you to rely more on intuition, and to call upon outside supports to bounce back from adversity.

Questions also arise when you are adapting. You may find yourself struggling to answer questions such as, "How am I going to deal with this latest dilemma?" "Who is going to be there for me through *this?*" "What do I do first?" "Will I ever feel good again?" "Haven't I suffered enough?"

At the point of adaptation—or at any point on the circle—fears and worries are normal. When questions like these arise, all you have to do is acknowledge the fears, doubts, and insecurities, and return to hopeful mindsets as often as you need to. As your intuition increases and your effective coping strategies improve, you will have more resilience to respond appropriately and effectively to your problems, to the needs and emotions of your children, and to the requirements of your own Self care.

As with all the positions in the cycle, you may go through effective adaptation many times as life events unfold. My own times in this position required more resilience than I ever imagined I could have. When I was first separated, the responsibilities and requirements for effective adaptation were physically and emotionally overwhelming.

My aunt offered insight and inspiration for growth toward the solid center of my true MRS.

PLAYING THE HAND YOU'RE DEALT: A STORY OF ADAPTATION

"Dov needs to 'find himself,'" I told Aunt Annie. "Where you can find me is home, bringing up two little girls by myself! I know *where* I am, but I no longer have a clue of *who* I am!"

Only fifteen years older, Annie was my aunt by marriage, and my close friend. Beautiful, intelligent, and wise, Annie seemed to know about relationships and life. Annie believed in being true to yourself, and I felt authentic when I was with her. Now, when I felt as if I were fragmenting into little pieces of my Self, I longed for Annie to tell me who I was and what to do about my life. But what she said wasn't what I wanted to hear.

"Bette, you have to play the hand you've been dealt," Annie said. "Life gives no guarantees. You've dealt with some big problems, and you are a strong woman."

No, I'm Humpty Dumpty! I thought.

"You have to face this deal, and you have the ability to make a good life. No one, not even a husband, can take *You* away from *You!*"

But I had no interest in my current hand. I wanted out of the game! I wanted Annie to tell me that someone else could *(would!)* do the hard stuff. I wanted her to have magic to take away my pain. Still, somewhere in me I knew she was right. I had to rely on *me* to put the pieces of my life, and my Self, together.

Despite Annie's reassurances that I was strong enough to solve my problems, I felt my identity and stability slipping away. I thought it might help if Annie shared how she had coped years before when she had left her husband and for a short while had lived in another state with her teenage daughter.

Annie told me how difficult it had been for her to be a single mother. In the end living on her own had been too overwhelming, and she'd gone back to her husband. Reuniting had been Annie's way of playing her hand—however, as scared as I was, I knew it was not meant to be mine. Despite how hard it was going to be to raise my children as a single mother, I knew intuitively that, despite sadness and fear, going back was not in the cards.

While one part of me railed against adapting to this deal, another, more intuitive part sensed that I needed to deal with this new way of life to become strong. I'd had a brief idea that single motherhood might open doors for me that might otherwise stay closed. Both parts of me were real, and I chose the one that resonated most strongly with my desire for Self development.

I took Annie's advice and started dealing, and adapting. I buried myself in my social work studies and doing all I could to effectively parent my daughters. As my journey evolved I had less contact with Annie, but the bond remained. It comforted me to know that Annie was a few years ahead of me, and that someday I would talk to her about how to adapt to adult children flying the stable nest I had worked so hard to feather.

However, the last time I did speak to Annie was about her own need for adaptation. Her husband had just died, and Annie was grieving and getting used to being a single mother again—now supporting her adult children in their loss, even as they supported her. Sadly, while putting her life together as a widow and as a single mother, Annie was struck and killed by a car.

In an attempt to come to grips with her death, I spoke with a friend who is a pastor. "Feel your sadness, and honor her life by the way you live yours," my friend counseled.

Her words reverberated with echoes of Annie's wisdom. Annie honored the feelings and encouraged the correct action based on authentic Self. She always advised me to stay open to what I could learn from what life dealt out.

It occurred to me that even in our different ways of playing our hands, I had learned that there is more than one way to be true to authentic Self. Annie taught me that there is no right answer, only action that is right for the time, for the deal, and for continuing the journey to MRS.

STRATEGIES FOR ACHIEVING EFFECTIVE ADAPTATION

- Trust that you can function appropriately and effectively as the head of your family.
- Create a toolkit of skills for effective parenting and creative management of stress.
- Use parenting skills, inner guidance, and outside supports to bounce back from change and adversity.
- Let go of victim thinking, and hold onto the belief that you can create a satisfying life.
- Believe that you deserve the right to take care of your Self.
- Co-parent with the other parent, as long as safety needs are met.
- Use inner wisdom in combination with clear thinking and effective actions to build your Responsive-resilience and Self-strength.

AN AFFIRMATION FOR EFFECTIVE ADAPTATION

I am able to discern the best choices for myself and for my children. I am able to mobilize the supports I need to live well and effectively. I am able to decide what is right to do in all my circumstances. I am able to develop and use skills to manage my life, and I trust that all forces in the universe are working toward my higher good and the good of my children. These truths add to the wisdom in my Authentic Self.

When single-mother life becomes stressful you may find that for a while you will move quickly around the circle, from identity to adaptation and back again. Eventually it will happen that you will touch down, and spend some time, in the stage of Restorative Stability.

GENERATING RESTORATIVE STABILITY

Restorative Stability is not an end, but another important point along your road to MRS. As you become more solid and whole you will pass through the Position of Restorative Stability many times. A major challenge in generating Restorative Stability is to integrate your positive Self-identity and your toolkit of strategies for effective adaptation into a well-functioning operation with tools you can use to cope or to correct course.

In the Position of Restorative Stability, you will find yourself feeling more whole, worrying less, and counting on Soul Mother Wisdom more. One helpful strategy is to memorize how you feel when you come around to this position. Then during other, more stressful times you can simply recall what it feels like to feel stable. The memory itself can reduce stress, make you feel better, and strengthen your connection to Soul Mother Wisdom.

RESTORING A SELF AND REBUILDING A LIFE: BARBARA'S STORY

Barbara's story is an outstanding example of how a single mother faces the challenge of restoring stability. You will be inspired by the way Barbara surmounted incredible adversity, recreated her identity, and rebuilt her life, quite literally from the ground up. As you read, I hope you will think about the resilience, strength, and courage in your own story.

"I became a single mother after a pressured year of renovating a house with my husband and some builders," Barbara told me. "We had a three-year-old son, and in the middle of the project I had my second child. Around that time I noticed that my husband seemed unhappy and angry a lot of the time. I thought it was stress over the renovation, but shortly after our second son was born, he told me he wanted to be with a woman he'd recently met.

"We separated when the baby was about three months old. After almost four and a half years of separation, and some attempts to work out things, we got divorced. And I had a new life as a single mother. It was a hard beginning, because it was abrupt and there was another woman. Shock—incredible disappointment—terrible feelings of abandonment. I had thought I was in a happy marriage. I was barely coming to grips with being the mother of two children, let alone being suddenly a single mother, alone with two babies.

"It was like the door closed in my face, and I saw ten more heavy leaden doors that I had to walk through. I wanted none of it. I was hurt, sad, and angry. There were moments when I was stunned by the realization of how much I was needed by my boys when I had so many needs myself, and so much ahead of me."

What Barbara faced behind those doors was what virtually all single mothers face, whether by choice or circumstance, as they create or re-create stability in their lives. Barbara had to renew her positive Self-identity as a whole person with an intact family, adapt effectively to changing roles and relationships, and manage a multitude of painful feelings while successfully parenting her children.

For starters, Barbara had to deal with her former husband. Dick wanted their boys to have a relationship with his new partner. But that was too fast for Barbara, and according to her, much too fast for the boys. Barbara didn't want her sons introduced to the woman so quickly. But wisely, she valued the relationship between the boys and their father, and wanted to do what she could to protect those bonds.

That meant negotiating shared parent time with her ex and his soon-to-be wife. It meant knowing what she could and what she could not control, such as saying "No" to something she felt wouldn't be in the boys' interest, or saying "Yes" to something that broke her heart. Barbara would need to reach into Soul Wisdom to balance her conflicting priorities—and soon, to deal with what else life was dealing out.

While Barbara was adapting to never-ending responsibility, financial worries, and unrelenting stress, her mother—her main emotional support—became terminally ill. After her mother's death, Barbara shared that she'd actually felt despair. While doing her best to stay emotionally and physically available to her boys and meet the requirements of her new life, Barbara felt overwhelmed. She was grieving for her marriage, for her mother, and for her "lost dreams."

However, due to a healthy dose of Responsive-resilience, Barbara was determined to adapt to these circumstances. She knew she would have to let go of the dream that Dick would come back. For the first couple months she worried and cried and talked to friends to figure out how to cope.

Then one day it came to her that she needed to give more to her children. After this insight she focused more energy and time on her boys. By trusting her intuition, Barbara moved into the position of recreating stability. She was learning that besides her knowledge, resourcefulness, and hard work, she needed to trust her wise inner voice to parent effectively while she remade her life. Soul Mother Wisdom was moving Barbara along her road to the true MRS of her solid Self.

Barbara now took other steps to put life back together. She prepared for a divorce, and renovated a rental apartment in her restored house. As she used ingenuity and inner guidance to cope and rebuild, Barbara was beginning to feel strong again. She recalled that time in our interview.

"I began building a rental apartment in the house. That was another heavy door to walk through. But when it was done, the rent would pay half my mortgage. Dick helped pay the mortgage for only three months, and six months after he left, my mother died. So I had to rely on myself to figure everything out, and fast.

"Eventually I started to enjoy my house and my life again. I was able to do things around the house to make it work for the boys and me. We had a fireplace, and I had an art space. After having been in total shock and disarray, it was my nest. I was afraid of having dreams, except for that house. It was the one stable thing I clung to through the first year. I was planning on raising the kids in that house. It was an incredible place."

Despite two major losses, Barbara was becoming stronger. Little did she know she would need the wholeness of MRS to deal with what was coming next.

Almost a year after Dick left, just before Christmas, through a freak accident—supposedly a spark from a builder's tool—Barbara's house, her nest with her apartment, all her belongings, and her mother's treasures, burned to the ground. Barbara was left in full despair. Now she had no dreams at all. And once again she had a difficult time addressing the emotional needs of the children.

However, as it had once before, Barbara's Soul Mother Wisdom came through and enabled her to re-stabilize her life.

"This time I went into therapy. As when Dick left, I had rushes of anxiety, but worse. It was too many losses. And the kids were really needing me. After the fire we stayed with friends, and then we moved into a horrible apartment. Everything was gone. But I knew the kids and I needed to be together. We put the beds together and slept in this huge bed, and we played and were just together. I think they were glad I wasn't renovating a house anymore.

"It was very hard, but there were also wonderful times. I allowed myself to feel vulnerable. There was something about this time that was deepening me, something that probably I didn't have strongly in my life before—the ability to just be in the moment with another person, in this case, my kids. I had been afraid of deeper feelings and afraid of closeness. Afraid of somebody asking something of me, and needing—really needing—me. But being able to be with my kids, even with all the heartache, and being able to talk about this with a couple of supportive friends, allowed me to realize that I was still whole.

"I was drawing on something inside of myself, and developing new skills. I was coming to know my Self. I knew I had to grow. I wanted to work through the anxiety to be there for my kids. They were the reasons I wasn't running away. I seemed to be discovering an inner wisdom that was leading me to decisions that were ultimately best for all of us. It was as if something in my true Self overrode the horror of so many tragic losses. It was as if some invisible, but *wise force* kept me making healthy choices."

There is much encouragement in Barbara's story. While the pain of loss and abandonment almost caused her to fall apart, the Soul Wisdom force of true MRS kept her together. Somehow, although she felt almost dysfunctional, Barbara found ways to stay connected to her boys and to her authentic Self.

Despite grief and fear, mature and resilient parts of Barbara's solid Self prevailed, allowing her recognize that she had strong parts of Self that could respond to problems in order to restore stability. She could build a new life.

Since that time Barbara has bought and renovated another house. She has established a career as an art therapist, and has gotten better at self care. A few years ago she remarried. Even now, with a former husband and two adolescent boys, there are still "single mother" issues, but Barbara asserts that her "tolerance is higher for truly being Me."

With assurance, Barbara asserts, "Single motherhood continues to teach me that I am a whole person with enough maturity to create a stable and satisfying life."

Through all her traumas, Barbara's connection to Soul Mother Wisdom allowed her to know what she needed to do. Maturity, resilience and Self-strength gave her the courage to do it!

STRATEGIES FOR RESTORING STABILITY

- Consistently hold your sense of Self-worth as a mother and as a whole person.
- Believe that inner wisdom can guide your responses in all situations.
- Continue to learn more about what you think, feel and do by understanding your goals and motivations.
- Trust that in your challenges are the opportunities that can inspire you to develop Meta-maturity, Responsive-resilience and Self-strength.
- Believe in the courage, creativity, and accomplishments in your story.
- Practice balancing your own needs with the needs of your children.
- Continue to cultivate outside supports.
- Maintain a no-blame appraisal of the areas in which you wish to grow into greater MRS.
- Continue to use a combination of strategies and inner wisdom to bounce back from difficult situations.
- Mobilize the courage within your Self to allow your children (where safety is met) to stay connected to branches of their family that may no longer be yours.
- Foster the ability to derive joy from your children and your life, with or without a partner.

With Restorative Stability you have created an effective operating system for facing life challenges. You are able to use your thoughts, emotions, and Soul Wisdom as guidance for making effective coping choices. Every dilemma you face makes you more able to solve the next problem.

Now you might like to take a moment to sit peacefully and use this affirmation for inspiration and guidance.

I affirm my wholeness and my connection to my deeper, wise Self.
Neither negativity, fears, nor other people's opinions have power over

me. I remain connected to my authentic Self. I am a mature, strong and resilient woman. I am able to hold myself together in one Peace even when I am afraid I am going to pieces. I trust that I am surrounded by healing energy that fills me with the strength and courage to press on. I open my mind to truth and inspiration. The guidance from my Soul provides insight for coping. I continue to find my true Soul nature. I allow only positive thoughts to have influence over me. I bathe in the love and wisdom of my True Self.

TIPS FOR EMPOWERMENT OF TRUE MRS

Growing into wholeness and wisdom takes time and practice. With the following tips you can further develop the qualities and practice the strategies of Meta-maturity, Responsive-resilience and Self-strength.

- Connect to MRS by noticing what you think, feel, and do. Noticing how you operate as you go about your life can give you insight into the parts of your Self that empower your wholeness, and can open access to Soul Wisdom.
- Be mindful of images and ideas that indicate where you might be in the cycle of achieving MRS. Such awareness offers choices for responding more effectively to problems, and for restoring stability. The more you recognize and utilize the qualities and strategies of each position of growing into MRS, the more your Soul Wisdom will be empowered.
- Ask yourself questions that make you think about your choices. For example:
    What part of me made that particular choice?
    What is my intention in responding like this?
    What was my motivation for responding like that?
- Use your senses to understand your authentic Self. For example, you can "see" choices in your mind's eye and follow them to an imagined conclusion in order to "see" which one might be most correct. You can "hear" the guidance from your inner voice. Sometimes even the sense of taste can be helpful. For example, if some idea leaves "a bad taste in your mouth," this is important information. Using your senses opens a strong connection to the wisdom of MRS.
- Continue to know parts of your true Self by paying attention to

what you're feeling, thinking, and doing. Knowing your parts creates wholeness. However, wholeness doesn't mean you'll be the same way all the time. As your Self-identify becomes more positive you'll become more aware of different aspects of Self operating in different situations, and will be more able to adapt effectively to events and restore stability when necessary.

- Pay attention to sensations that arise in your body. Your awareness is not just in your head—it is also in your body. If your stomach turns when considering a certain option, you're receiving an important message. Do your hands get clammy thinking about a possible solution? Inner wise guidance can actually be intuited from body sensations, and the more you pay attention, the more you can come to recognize the body messages that guide you closer to true MRS.

- Trust your emotions. As you recognize and experience emotions on your journey through the positions of true MRS, you may find that although feelings come and go, some feelings are more predominant at particular points. For example, in the stage of Forming a Positive Identity you may feel vulnerable much of the time. In the stage of Effective Adaptation you may have insecurities and fears. Trusting that your feelings are okay can help you feel more solid. It's normal to sometimes feel shaky as you grow. Remember, you don't have to always feel okay to be okay! This reassurance can relieve anxiety and promote the inner peace that can come with Soul Mother Wisdom.

IDEAS FOR REFLECTION AND INSIGHT: GOING AROUND THE CIRCLE IN ONE "PEACE"

As you travel each stage, you will be learning to tolerate the emotional discomfort that comes with the requirements of changing circumstances. Over time, as you deal with your thoughts, emotions, and responses in each stage you will strengthen and consolidate your belief in your identity as a strong woman heading an intact family. You will acquire greater trust in your ability to adapt to whatever life deals out, and your solid core of Authentic Self will hold you together in one peace.

What you succeed in accomplishing as you journey to MRS can help you believe in yourself. Affirm your accomplishments, even the ones that seem small! Think about problems you've resolved. What resources did you use? Then ask yourself, "What resources do I have now that I didn't have before? What are the challenges I am now facing, and what newly acquired skills do I have to resolve them?"

As you continue to cope with what life deals out, Meta-maturity, Responsive-resilience and Self-strength will become the solid central core of your wholeness and wisdom. You will find that with true MRS confusion can fade, insights can sharpen, and solutions can become clearer. Your solid Self will become more stable, and you will come to be able to accomplish the critical tasks of being a single mother. You can now with confidence affirm:

Every day in every way, I am making my life work! I am becoming a strong, mature, resilient, wise woman, and an effective single mother!

PAGES FOR JOURNALING

Writing can help you to bring forth your inner voice and nourish your inner spirit. As you jot down your thoughts, feelings, and insights, remember to include memories of your strongest and most authentic moments.

You might want to make up a list of key qualities of true MRS, as you see them. You can also describe the many ways the inner force of Soul Mother Wisdom is guiding you into Meta-maturity, Responsive resilience and Self-strength.

As you read what you've written, you can derive insight into your experiences and discover the gifts you have been given. Sit, reflect, breathe, intuit, write, and read. The information from your Soul Wisdom will come and will show you the way to more confidence in your solid Self.

Your journal can help you come to a better understanding of your choices and find new meaning in your personal quest for the wholeness and wisdom that lives at the center of your authentic Self.

INSIGHT FOUR

With Coping Power You Can Beat Your Stress

"Stress closes the door to deep knowing. You don't see what is possible unless you can see what you fear."

SINGLE MOTHER, 2007

BECOMING A STRESS BEATER

In the life of a single mother, stress can build up. When you have to take care of a sick baby—arrange a toddler's birthday party—plan supper—clean the house—get the car fixed—help your eight-year-old with math—talk about money with the other parent—call the doctor—call your mother—get a lawyer—and then get to work, I suspect you know more than you want to know about stress. Being a single mother can involve stressors that are overlapping, overwhelming, and at times, over the top.

But knowing how to cope with multiple stressful situations and keep your sanity at the same time is another story. Let's consider some established facts.

- Health, both physical and mental, can improve when stress is managed effectively at least most of the time.
- Coping effectively with stress can reduce the risk of developing physical illnesses and emotional problems such as anxiety and depression.

- Managing stress effectively can increase the potential for inner peace and Self-awareness.
- Effective stress management strategies are more likely to lead to more effective parenting strategies.
- Lowering parental stress has the potential to positively affect children's stress.
- Children have more favorable behavioral and emotional outcomes when parents are coping effectively with their own stressors.
- Techniques and strategies for managing stress are similar to those used for accessing intuitive knowing.

Using stress-beating strategies can increase your resilience, build your Self-strength, improve your parenting and problem-solving skills, and open your channel to Soul Mother Wisdom. For these reasons, doesn't it make sense to beat stress before it beats you?

To begin the process of developing your stress-beating power, it might be helpful to get an idea of your past and current experiences of successful coping as a single mother and as a person. You might want to take a moment to think about the stressors you've faced, and the ways in which you've coped with them. Thinking about the outcomes that have occurred can show you where your strategies are most useful and where you want to increase or improve your coping power.

How have your thoughts and emotions affected your choices?
How effective have been your coping choices?
How would you describe your typical coping style?
What are your current stressors?
What can you learn from past coping choices that can help you beat stress today?

Building your coping power requires an adequate amount of Meta-maturity, Responsive-resilience and Self-strength. In turn, as you cope more effectively with stress you will also build the powerful qualities of your true MRS.

In learning how to unleash your coping power, it's worth considering the various choices you have for beating stress. Let's continue by focusing on some of my favorite ideas and strategies for beating stress before it beats you.

BEAT STRESS WITH
RELAXATION/MEDITATION SKILLS

Relaxation and meditation are proven to be effective methods for changing stress into the "relaxation response," as defined by Herbert Benson, M.D., author of the book by the same name. When relaxation techniques and mediation practices are used in combination with realistic thinking and positive affirmations, the potential to feel better and cope better is enhanced.

If you would like to experience the enjoyment of relaxation and the morale boost of balanced, upbeat thinking, you might like to try the following exercise.

> Taking a gentle breath and continuing to breathe slowly and rhythmically, settle into a comfortable place and a space of comfort within your Self.
>
> Feel and imagine your body relaxing. Trust that whatever you experience is right for you. If negative thoughts arise, you can let them come and go. There is no need to grab onto them or push them away.
>
> To enter a deeper state of relaxation, you can count from ten to one. At the count of one you will feel more deeply relaxed.
>
> Now, as you breathe normally, call to mind a place that is pleasant for you. It can be a familiar place or one you imagine. Imagine experiencing this place with your senses. See the sights, smell the smells, hear the sounds, and feel textures that you find in your special place.
>
> If you find other people there, you can welcome them or send them away. If you wish to speak with them, you might ask them if they have insights and wisdom for you. Enjoy your time as if you are truly visiting.
>
> Spend a few moments in your special place, and when you are ready, return to the time and place of the present moment, affirming that when you reorient you will be relaxed and peaceful and in perfect health, bringing back any wisdom you may need for coping with your stress and your life.
>
> If you wish, you can memorize the feeling of relaxation and come back to it any time you wish some stress relief.

As part of this exercise, you can also choose to mentally visualize coping choices and imagine the possible outcomes of each option. As you reflect upon potential consequences, your inner wisdom will provide information to help you take action with the greatest potential for success.

COPE MORE EFFECTIVELY WITH THE LEMON SOLUTION

Stress management experts point out that both real and imagined stressors can prime your body's stress reactions. A simple exercise can demonstrate this mental power. I call it the Lemon Effect.

> Bring to mind a picture of a juicy yellow lemon. Now, imagine cutting it open and sucking on a slice. Do your salivary glands tingle? If so, you're experiencing the way your mind can bring about a physical response.
>
> If it doesn't happen the first time, try it again. Or how about this? Bring to mind your most favorite meal, and see what happens.

The stress-beating importance of the Lemon Effect is that the effect goes beyond the lemon. Because worry about stress can bring about the stress response, even thinking about something stressful causes your body and your emotions to respond as if that something was actually taking place. This stress response, also referred to as the fight-or-flight response, is nature's way of preparing all animals to deal with danger or the threat of danger.

The difference between other animals and us is that we worry and they don't. For humans, stress—real or imagined—causes your body to get you ready to fight or flee.

Some stress management experts say, "When you can't fight and you can't flee, then flow." I've named the "flow" option the Lemon Solution. To understand how you can "flow" to beat stress, you can try a different exercise that will utilize the Lemon Solution.

> This time bring to mind an actual stressor or an imagined stressor (something that worries you). What thoughts come to mind? What do you notice in your body?
>
> Do your muscles tighten? Does your tummy feel funny? Do you feel sweaty, tingly, or confused? What emotions arise in you?
>
> It's possible to bring about the physical aspects of stress just by

thinking about something stressful!

Now, as you're taking a couple of gentle, easy breaths, imagine that this same stressor is now resolved. There's no need to figure out how you resolved it, although that wisdom may come. Just notice how you feel.

Spend a few seconds or minutes with the sensations of these new feelings. You may feel your body go into a more peaceful place as the stress symptoms subside.

Any time the stress feelings come back, return to the Lemon Solution feelings. Your body and mind know the difference.

Sometimes the solutions actually come during this type of exercise. Sometimes they come later. But you may be surprised at how the Lemon Solution can change the sensations of the *feelings*, which in turn changes your body's stress response. When you "flow" you reduce the bodily wear and tear of the physiology of stress, which then provides health benefits for your body and for your mind. It takes a little practice to see how well this works, but with a few attempts you might be amazed at how much better you can feel.

You've probably heard the expression, "When life gives you lemons, make lemonade." This is actually a great way to describe how the Lemon Solution can beat stress.

The ABCs and DEFGs can further explain the stress-beating power that is unleashed when you manage your mind.

THE ABCS (AND DEFGS) OF BEATING STRESS

Aggravation, Beliefs and Consequences

A. Stress gets Activated when *you* get Aggravated by an actual or imagined situation. Even painful memories can be aggravating events. Most people believe that you cannot control your thoughts, but actually you can. Remember the Lemon Effect and the Lemon Solution?

B. Beliefs influence thinking. When beliefs are based in disaster thinking, stress may result and may compromise Responsive-resilience, an important source of coping power. Becoming aware of underlying beliefs gives you an edge in heading off the mental, physical, or emotional factors in stress and its cousin, burnout. When you know what you think, you have the opportunity to use mind power to change your thoughts and reduce your stress.

C. You may not always be able to Control your emotions, but you can Choose how you think, and how you act. Your thinking and action Choices have Consequences that can Change your emotional state for the better and resolve stress more readily.

"Disastranautics," Emotions, Fear, and "The Gobble"

D. Distorted thinking can trap you and steal your peace. Too much time spent struggling with negative and distorted thoughts can create "Disastranautics," those quick blast-offs into catastrophic thinking that create high-volume stress. *Feeling Good* by David Burns, M.D. is a good reference for learning more about distorted thinking and its effects.

E. & F. Emotions such as Fear and resentment may arise from distorted thinking, and usually increase stress. Recognizing and changing distorted thoughts has the power to inspire coping choices that effectively reduce stress. Some refer to distorted thinking as "stinking thinking." My Alanon sponsor calls it "gobbledygook," or "The Gobble."

G. The Gobble can easily get you caught in "thinking traps" of distortion that undermine your Self-strength, muddy your ability to see effective solutions, and increase the time you spend with an activated stress response.

Following are a few of my "favorite" thinking traps. Do you recognize any?

ALL OR NOTHING

All-or-nothing thinking, good/bad thinking, is absolutist. This trap limits the ability to think clearly and the abilities to be flexible, to be resilient, or to reach a compromise. All-or-nothing thinking interferes with Meta-maturity, that quality of true MRS which enables you to take into account the larger picture. Avoid this trap by catching yourself thinking in absolute terms and then balance it out.

THE BLAME GAME

Thinking in terms of "it's all your fault" or "It's all *my* fault" puts you at risk for being unable to clearly and realistically assess the complexities of a situation. This trap can lead to persistent stress, low Self-esteem, resentment, diminished resilience, and anxiety.

Avoid this trap by being aware of victim thinking or too much guilt for things not in your control.

THE CRYSTAL BALL

Thinking you know the future or know what someone else is thinking puts you at risk for acting as if you have a crystal ball and know what someone else feels or is going to do. Even if you might be correct, this trap causes you to behave from assumptions rather than reality. To avoid this trap, notice your thinking and check out your assumptions with the appropriate person.

PERSONALIZING

The Blame Game and The Crystal Ball can result in your believing that what people do or say is somehow related to you. This trap can lead to unrealistic comparisons to others, holding other people responsible for your hurt or mistakes, or overly blaming yourself for your problems. Too much blame may limit crucial qualities of MRS such as Responsive-resilience or Self-strength. Avoid this trap by realizing that not all roads end up at your door.

SHOULDING

"Shoulding" is a belief system involving rules that you or others are "supposed" to think and behave in certain ways. When you have such rules, whether you know you do or not, you are at risk of trying to be right instead of peaceful. The late great psychologist Albert Ellis referred to this trap as "musterbation." To avoid "shoulding" on yourself, notice when "should" or its variations ("have to," "ought to," "must") appear in your thoughts. Change these to "want" or "want to" and notice the difference.

"WHAT IF" AND "IF ONLY"

"What If" and "If Only" thinking involves the belief that others should, and will, change to suit you *if only* you find the right way to get them to do it. "What If" and "If Only" are first cousins of "shoulding" in the family of peace-of-mind stealers. These traps can cause resentment, fear, anxiety, and victim thinking, and compromise your ability to assess a situation clearly. They put you at risk of becoming a "disastranaut." To avoid these traps, be realistic about what you can and cannot control.

When you recognize that you're stuck in a thinking trap, you may try my method. I say *"gobble, gobble, gobble"* very fast to myself (or out loud!) This makes me laugh, which blocks my negative thinking, physiologically reduces the stress hormones, and highlights the realization that I can change my thinking.

Once you become aware of your thinking traps, you can use the Lemon Solution to get free. Climbing out is worth it. It just takes willingness—and, as always, a little practice.

As you practice getting free of thinking traps and other gobbled thinking, you might ask yourself these questions:

What thoughts and feelings came up?
What role did my thoughts and feelings play in causing stress?
Did a thinking trap play a role in how I felt?
What coping decisions did I make? What were the consequences?
How well did my decisions reduce stress?

BEAT THE STRESS OF DISTORTED THINKING

Unrelenting distorted thinking can be exhausting. It can launch you into chronic stress, fill you with sour emotions, steal your peace of mind, and make you a disastranaut.

As a single mom rearing two little kids, I was often a disastranaut. I constantly feared that I might get sick, that the kids would get sick, and/or that I might lose what I had worked so hard to build. When the time came to send my older daughter to college—and simultaneously buy my house from Dov's widow—I spent days fearing the worst before my resilience kicked in.

My worries and fears produced disaster thinking: "I can't do this! I don't have what it takes. I'm definitely not strong enough. I can't believe this is happening. I'm ruined." The intense stress of my disastranautics cycled me back to fear of getting sick. And the stress of my negative thinking made it more likely!

Fortunately, I had enough stress management knowledge to realize that I didn't want to rob my precious energy with negative Self talk. Despite the fact that part of me really thought I might go under, I told myself "I can" when the disastranaut part of me said "You can't." The outcome was that I could and I did.

"Wait!" you say. "You can't pretend things are great when they aren't!" True enough, and of course I did have serious problems, as all single mothers do. But excess focus on negatives can lead to the damaging stress of disaster thinking.

The solution is to *accept the reality of a difficult situation,* choose stress-reduction strategies such as the Lemon Solution, a revision of your beliefs, and/or time spent in your healing room. Remember to use positive affirmations, seek professional support as needed, or find a friend who can give you a good pep talk.

However, if underneath the pep lurk anger, fear, and resentment, your thinking will still stink. Unrecognized stress can darken the Soul's inner knowing and make it harder for you to make effective choices. Sweeping out the musty, dark corners of negative thinking while drawing on Self-strength and Responsive-resilience can lead to clear thinking that can reduce stress and open the door to Soul Mother Wisdom.

You can use the following affirmation to correct your thinking:

My story reveals courage and wisdom that empowers my current decisions. In my story I find the seeds and essentials for the blossoming of maturity, resilience, and strength. As I stay aware of what I am thinking and feeling, Soul Mother Wisdom shows me the way to effective choices for my Self and for my children.

Now, check out a few simple questions to see if you might be at risk for becoming a disastranaut.

Do you blast off into catastrophic thinking when faced with a stressor?
Are you spending time thinking, "Why me?
Are you secretly telling yourself "Life sucks, and then you die?"
Does your digestion change after weeks of thinking someone else makes you sick?
Are you thinking thoughts like, "I'm not good enough, smart

enough, pretty enough, sexy enough, _____ enough?"

There's no need to stress out if you found you have some of these signs. Given what single mothers have to cope with, all single mothers have negative or distorted thoughts at times.

When I was in the midst of difficult times, it helped to remember that fears are normal and that I could trust that, despite my fears, I could prevail without becoming miserable or sick. It also helped to reach into Soul Wisdom to find solutions.

FIND STRESS-BEATING POWER IN YOUR STORY

When your mental dialogue becomes chronically negative, you most likely will get stressed. But there is hope! One way to beat chronic stress and keep yourself from becoming a disastranaut is to reflect upon the positive experiences in your story. Your accomplishments can give you courage and inspire confidence in your ability to cope.

It's relatively simple to do this. Think about past stressors you've experienced and what Self-resources and Self-support network resources helped you cope. You might be surprised to find a particular episode from your story that shows your resilience and Self-strength. Each successful coping experience, no matter how small, can increase your courage and deepen your wisdom. Those episodes that resolve less satisfactorily than you might have wished can also help you to evaluate, learn, and grow.

For example, that August night when Dov died, a new chapter of my single mother story began and beckoned me to rely on resilience, wisdom, and Self-strength. I had thought the worst was over. I had survived the anguish of divorce, made it through the rigors of social work school, and had landed a job that was low paying but perfect. I thought that I was managing the stress of single motherhood reasonably well. However, this new episode brought forth new difficulties that would move me to learn and grow in ways I had never imagined.

Now Dov's words, "It's okay," became a prophecy I will never forget, and gave meaning to my story that only Soul Wisdom could truly fathom. In the moment when I learned he had died, I knew my single mother life was forever changed. Now I was the only living parent, and they were "all mine."

Although in those first days of disbelief I had no idea how I would manage the complexities ahead, some courageous and comforting part of myself made its way into my awareness over the next few weeks. Despite the numbness of disbelief, I sensed a strand of Self-strength. Although stress soared to new heights, Soul Wisdom cautioned me to spare my children as much as possible from my fear and grief. I knew the next chapters wouldn't be easy, but I promised myself that I would prevail and that we three would be okay.

Experts agree that one of the most effective stress management tools is taking action. After Dov died, and I regained my ability to function, I took actions that reduced my stress and affirmed that I could cope. Wise knowing again cautioned me to spare my children as much stress as I could. Despite what lay ahead, I promised myself to do whatever it would take to keep them safe and launch them into adulthood with as little damage as possible to their vulnerable psyches.

And for the most part, we were okay. Then on the day that Dov's father announced the end of money from Dov's estate and told me that I would have to buy our house, I determined once more not to go under. I pledged to keep us stable. I worked hard to build my practice, fought for the house, and continued to learn new ways to manage stress.

In Boston I developed the stress management courses that I still teach, and using the same techniques I was able to keep from falling apart. However, at one point during that period I developed an anxiety disorder—a full-blown phobia of crossing bridges. Fortunately my curiosity about the nature of stress and coping, and yet another good therapist, helped me understand that my phobia might be a metaphor for my fear of crossing a life bridge into unknown and frightening territory.

Uncovering this meaning in my story helped resolve the phobia, and the resulting Self-awareness deepened my connection to Soul Mother Wisdom and increased my dedication to help others deal with stress. During that difficult and scary time, I found a poem that inspired me to trust that I had the courage to cross into the next phase of my single mother life.

CROSSING A CREEK
BY MARTHA COURTOT

crossing a creek
requires 3 things:

a certain serenity of mind
bare feet
and a sure trust
that the snake we know
slides silently
underwater
just beyond our vision
will choose to ignore
the flesh
that cuts through
its territory
and we *will* pass through

some people think crossing a creek
is easy
but I say this—

all crossings are hard
whether creeks, mountains
or into other lives

and we must always believe
in the snakes at our feet
just out of our vision

and we must practice believing
we *will* come through.

BOOST YOUR COPING POWER
WITH THE SOLVE METHOD

The SOLVE Method is a five-step approach to effective problem solving that primes the coping power of Soul Wisdom with the concepts of the ABCDEFGs of stress. Practicing the SOLVE Method can help you more easily find solutions, and in many cases lower your stress level sooner. Although the SOLVE steps are pointed out as a linear progression, they may happen simultaneously, or in bunches.

S–Stilling the mind. In preparation for SOLVE-ing, get comfortable and still your mind in any way you choose, including formal meditation. Take one or two gentle breaths, and then allow your breathing to follow its natural, rhythmic pattern. As thoughts pass through your mind you can gently let them come in and go out.

O–Opening the mind. Opening to information from any sense or source prepares the mind for solutions. As you gently reflect upon your problem, notice the thoughts, emotions, and sensations associated with the issue. What comes to you may or may not be what you expected, and may not be specific.

You may see images, sense metaphoric symbols, realize new ideas, or intuit something you may or may not immediately understand. Just be with your thoughts as they come in and go out. There's no need to force a solution. Some practitioners of methods like SOLVE suggest that just feeling the relief you will feel when the problem is solved, regardless of the actual solution, is an effective stress reducer. You can apply this step any time in the process, and as many times as you wish.

L–Letting Go. As you relax, let go of the mental stress of negative emotions, or "gobble," by breathing out tension anywhere in your body. Imagine tension being released through the skin, the top of your head, the bottoms of your feet, or in any other way you choose. Some refer to this process as "emptying the mind." Thoughts will still come—the idea is to just continue noticing feelings, thoughts, and sensations. Some may contain wisps of meaning and wisdom that you can assess later. Letting go of self-inflicted pressure to find a solution actually allows the mind to become more receptive to ideas, and tends to reduce stress.

V–Verifying. The goal in Verifying is the wisdom to know which ideas and solutions are right for you. To verify, reflect on what you receive in the Opening and Letting Go steps and consider what the information might mean to you. It helps to pay attention to the realities of your situation and to your feelings as well as to your intuition. As you reflect, you may be surprised at what's revealed. Although you may not understand all the meanings right away, you can begin to distinguish the intuitive aspects of Soul Wisdom. To help "verify" you can also talk with a trusted friend, therapist, or clergy person.

E–Evaluating. Evaluating is about considering your coping choices and what you wish a solution to achieve. Although evaluating is a "last step," it is also always an ongoing step in the SOLVE process. Get as honest with yourself as you can about your motivations and intentions for an outcome. What do you really want? Think about what might be some positive or negative consequences of a particular choice. When you feel ready, choose a solution. And act upon it.

After taking action, evaluate again. How did your choices work? Was the problem satisfactorily resolved, or was it a step toward resolution? An honest evaluation of outcomes and consequences can help you learn more about your coping style and more about your Self. Careful evaluation before and after and even during a particular situation will yield information that can help further refine your coping power.

Solutions sometimes come in parts and small pieces. One single mother using the SOLVE method to resolve some painful feelings about her adult child's choices didn't find an ultimate solution, but discovered a route to more inner peace. What came to her in the process was a vision of her maternal grandmother. Her realization that Gram had coped successfully with a dilemma similar to hers gave her hope for further explorations into the realm of inner wisdom.

Now, let me tell you how several years ago I used the SOLVE method to cope with a difficult dilemma of my own.

When I was preparing to move to Maine, my former in-laws asked to buy my drum set for their grandson, my children's half-brother. (My short "career" as a drummer is another story.) Because they were offering much less than what the drums were worth, the pilot light of resentment flared, and heated up the stress of old hurts and current confusion.

However, it also felt petty to haggle over the price knowing that it was not really the money, but the emotions that were the issue. Feeling the stress of my mixed feelings, I turned to the SOLVE process for relief. Almost instantly, a surprising solution came to me. Soul Wisdom informed me that when it came to stress, the one paying a price was me! When it came to relief from resentment and confusion, the solution had nothing to do with my former in-laws, and everything to do with me. Soul Wisdom told me that gifting the drums to my children's brother was the correct action.

Once I knew what to do, my negative feelings vanished. In Verifying, I realized this solution felt correct. In Evaluating, I realized that by giving the drums I let go of some of the resentment, which was causing my stress. The payment I received for my gift was the relief of forgiveness and a boost for my mental peace.

FIND COPING POWER IN OTHERS' STORIES

We can learn about beating stress from the stories of other single mothers whose courage and strength give us a model for Responsive-resilience and Self-strength. I am fortunate to have had several important single mother models along my journey. One of these was Tanya. Her story is a profile in true MRS.

POWER WOMAN—THE STORY OF TANYA

The last time I saw Tanya she was dying.

"Tanya was a powerful woman," her cousin said, looking as sad as I was feeling.

How could Tanya, who had been my rock for so many years of single motherhood, be on her death-bed? Tanya had been a resilient woman. She had moved from one state to another with the boys she raised virtually single-handedly. She had survived two divorces and the death of her children's biological father, and while managing all that she had written textbooks for teaching English as a second language. In addition, she had held demanding positions in a couple of publishing companies. Tanya had seen the twin towers fall and for the past three years had battled brain cancer. For a while it looked like she was winning.

Yes, Tanya was a Power Woman.

As I stood holding Tanya's familiar hand, memories flooded my mind. Tanya's first husband, Brett, had been friends with Dov in high school. When we first met pre-babies, Tanya and I were young wives and teachers. Almost instantly, we became friends.

A fantastic mother, gardener, and teacher, Tanya was writing textbooks before she was thirty. I envied Tanya's professional accomplishments, as well as her confidence. But Tanya never bragged about her successes. Rather, she encouraged me to believe in myself, achieve my own goals, and write my book.

Eventually both Tanya and I divorced, and our friendship morphed from buddies' wives to a strong support network of two single mothers. We bonded more deeply within the sisterhood of shared struggles, chronic exhaustion, and the determination to see our children thrive.

Eventually Tanya's work and her roots pulled her from New England back to her beloved Bronx. Now Tanya was near her mother, who could take care of the boys as Tanya traveled the world for her work. Despite her travels, Tanya saw to it that the children completed higher education and had the foundations to become the successful men they have come to be.

During those years we spoke often, visited as much as we could, and both remarried. But Tanya's second marriage did not survive the problems of the blended family. Divorced again, Tanya was discouraged, but, as always, remained devoted to her sons.

Then Tanya was diagnosed with cancer.

"I can't believe it," Tanya told me right after she got the news. "I have a brain tumor. What else can I possibly have to deal with?"

"This is awful news," I said. "But Tanya, you have always been strong, and I know how determined you can be."

"I don't feel strong anymore," my friend lamented. "But I'll do what I have to, as I always have."

And Tanya did do what she had to, courageously, until the cancer won.

Standing by Tanya's deathbed, hoping she could hear me, I spoke to her for the last time. "Tanya, girlfriend," I said, "you have done a really good job. The boys are good men, and have wonderful families now. Your mission is complete. We never did take the trip around the world we said we'd take when the kids grew up. But, my dear friend, you did go around the world, and gave so much to so many.

"And I am doing what you always said you knew I could. I'm writing the book for women like us, who are doing the hardest job in the world. I want to let them know that we did it, and they can do it too, even in tough times. Now it's time for you to rest. Your work is done."

Tanya couldn't respond, but intuitively I know she heard me. In my mind I "heard" her say, "Keep on going, Bette. I always knew you would do it, and I will always be with you."

And this is the most amazing part—I could feel Tanya's words. And even as her physical strength ebbed, I could feel the power of her inner will and her strong sense of doing what must be done. And I felt her "power" flow into me.

Before visiting Tanya, I myself had been sick. For several weeks I had felt tired, listless, and unmotivated. But when I left Tanya's bedside, I was reenergized in a way I hadn't been for years.

Tanya had always been there for me with wisdom, love, and encouraging words. Now it was as if I had taken her courage, wisdom, and strength into me one more time. This time they would need to last forever.

As Tanya might herself have said to me, I say this to you, single mother. *You, too, are a power woman.*

Single mothers have an amazing gift of maturity, resilience, and strength to share with each other. We can inspire one another with the same courage and belief in ourselves that Tanya gave to me.

TIPS FOR BEATING STRESS WITH COPING POWER

- **Know the factors involved in managing stress.** A healthy diet, adequate exercise, and enough sleep (we know this one is tough for single moms!) and supportive social networks add to the effective management of stress. It's not always easy to be on top of everything, but to the extent possible, work toward more healthy eating, more balanced thinking, adequate rest, peer support, and some time spent laughing.

- **Become familiar with the coping power of your mind.** Both people and animals have emergencies, but once animals fight or flee, they don't worry about the next crisis. People worry. Because of the Lemon Effect, the worry itself can affect how you feel, which will then affect other thoughts and feelings. Thinking and feeling combinations lead to effective or non-effective coping choices. By paying attention to the inner voice that is not garbled or gobbled, you will be able to access insights for more effective solutions.

- **Reflect on the strength in your own story and the stories of others to help boost your stress-beating and coping power.**
  How does your story reveal resilience and strength?
  What have you learned from seeing how others cope?
  Who in your life appears to have the wisdom you would like to have?
  With whom do you verify your ideas about solutions to your problems?
  Which coping choices have taught you the most about your Self?
  Which methods of relaxation and meditation have worked best for you?

- **Laugh!** It's very good for relieving the stress response, good for uplifting your spirits, and good for your Soul.

IDEAS FOR REFLECTION AND INSIGHT: THE NATURE OF STRESS AND THE POWER OF COPING

The word "stress" has a dual meaning. When it refers to a circumstance or situation that requires you to respond in some way, it's called a "stressor." The feeling you feel when you have a stressor is also referred to as stress, or sometimes as "stressed out." In other words, a stressor causes stress that makes you feel stressed!

Stressors, as well as your stressed-out feelings, can result from either pleasant or unpleasant situations. For example, going through a divorce or beginning a new relationship can cause stress. When a stressor comes from a positive source, it's called "eustress." When from a negative source, it's called "distress." You probably know quite a bit about the latter.

While some stressors are more severe than others, as in Barbara's story, the severity of your stress depends partly on what you're thinking, feeling, and believing about the stressor. Your thoughts, emotions, and beliefs affect the severity of the stressor and your response to it.

Past experiences influence how stressed you feel, and what coping choices you make. The usual or habitual way you cope is called your "coping style." The Evaluation step of SOLVE can help you assess how effective your coping choices and your coping style are in reducing your stress. The degree of success can reduce or, in some cases, even ramp up your stress.

Some coping choices and styles appear to lower stress because they make you feel better in the short-term. However, in the long run some choices—such as too many cigarettes or too much alcohol—have the potential to increase stress by causing other problems over time. While we cannot prevent all stress, the most successful coping choices and styles boost your skills for more successful parenting and more satisfying living by beating stress in the short and long term.

In his book *The Stress of Life,* Hans Selye offers a clear explanation of the effects of stress and the role that coping choices play in increasing or reducing the effects of stress.

Selye identifies three stages in a cycle of stress he labels the "General Adaptation Syndrome"—the Alarm Stage, the Adaptation Stage, and the Stage of Exhaustion. It's easy for me to remember the GAS Syndrome because stress can give you gas! Here's how it works.

In the Alarm Stage a real (or imagined) stressor brings on a physiological response characterized by changes in your body such as increased respiration, higher blood pressure, a faster heart rate and an influx of sugar into your bloodstream. These and other physiological effects have been termed "the stress response" by Dr. Herbert Benson, author of the book *The Relaxation Response.*

In Selye's explanation, the Alarm Stage does not necessarily mean crisis (though it could), but rather that a stress response has been activated by a stressor and the changes in physiology alert you that a coping choice is needed. The coping choice made in response to the "alarm" will be influenced by your thinking and your emotions, as well as by your coping style. Successful coping choices limit or stop the stress response.

One key to resolving stress in the Alarm Stage is to think through a problem clearly enough to take action that will be effective. Because so many problems have distorted thinking components, in many cases tweaking your thinking is all that is required to solve a problem and thus reduce your stress. The SOLVE Method can help with that.

While small doses of stress in the "alarm" phase are normal, and usually cause no long-term problems when resolved relatively quickly, some coping choices, though they make you feel good temporarily, can put you at risk for chronic stress because they do not always fully resolve the stress response.

When the stress response remains activated for too long, or you experience too many unresolved or partially resolved "alarms," your body becomes used to living with higher levels of the physiological components of stress, which leads to the Adaptation Stage, in which physical or emotional problems can begin to develop.

In the Adaptation Stage, you have become used to elevated blood pressure, higher levels of stomach acid, an increase in your blood sugar, or a chronic overflow of stress hormones being released into your bloodstream, often without realizing it. Physiological factors such as these can lead to chronic anxiety, depressed feelings, and a variety of physical problems, as well as a decrease in your energy. Ironically, in the Adaptation Stage, when you most need energy to cope, your coping energy is less. You may not even realize that unresolved stress has caused problems until you enter the Stage of Exhaustion, which is also often called "burnout."

It is in the Stage of Exhaustion that signs of chronic stress become more visible and more noticeable. While it's preferable to recognize the beginnings of symptoms earlier, it's possible to manage stress at any point in the GAS cycle. To help you become more aware, let's take a look at some of the signs and signals of stress. You may be familiar with some of these, and you may also have some that are not on the list.

Physical Symptoms

Headaches, indigestion and stomachaches, sleep disturbances, dizziness, back pain, tight neck and shoulders, heart palpitations, restlessness, chronic body aches, chronic fatigue, recurring respiratory problems.

Emotional Symptoms

Weepiness and crying, depression, nervousness, anxiety, boredom, feeling of meaninglessness, irritability, feeling stuck, feeling overwhelmed, overly angry, unhappy, easily hurt or upset, panicky, easily agitated.

Relationship Symptoms

Intolerance of others, resentments, blaming, lashing out, excessive partying, promiscuity, nagging distrust of others, using people, avoiding people, irritability, being overly critical.

Behavior Symptoms

Teeth grinding, excessive use of substances, compulsive eating, no appetite, inability to get things done, excessive use of caffeine, nicotine, alcohol, drugs, bingeing, purging, fear of going out, excessive need to control, avoidance of responsibility.

Spiritual Symptoms

Sense of emptiness, loss of faith, loss of meaning, doubt, martyrdom, looking for magic, loss of direction, apathy, inability to forgive.

Mental Symptoms

Negative thinking, victim thinking, confusion, difficulty concentrating, loss of focus, loss of interest in usual things.

Although it is desirable to resolve as much stress as possible in the Alarm Stage, it is never too early—or too late—to recognize stress symptoms and apply coping strategies to minimize their problematic potentials. For resolving stress at any point, your mind may be your most powerful tool.

Managing stress is a process, and you can become more adept at heading it off at the pass sooner. When you flow into the powerful intuitive dimension of your mind, you will find new ways to ease your stress, calm your worries, and acquire the wisdom for solving your problems.

By practicing the stress-beating techniques in this chapter, and other effective strategies you may discover, you will be able to differentiate distorted thinking from the wisdom of authentic Self, create powerful coping solutions that work, and continue to nourish the wise inner voice of Soul Mother Wisdom.

The following story, shared with me by a very wise single mother, seems to bring these ideas to life.

An elderly Cherokee Native American was teaching his grandchildren about life. He said to them, "A fight is going on inside me. It is a terrible fight, and it is between two wolves.

"One wolf is evil—he is fear, anger, envy, sorrow, regret, greed, arrogance, self-pity, guilt, resentment, inferiority, lies, false pride, competition, superiority, and ego. The other is good—he is joy, peace, love, hope, sharing, serenity, humility, kindness, benevolence, friendship, empathy, generosity, truth, compassion and faith.

"This same fight is going on inside you," he said, "and inside every other person, too."

They thought about it for a minute, and then one child asked his grandfather, "Which wolf will win?"

The old Cherokee simply replied, "The one you feed."

Pages for Journaling

Here you can write about your stressors, your coping choices, and how you are developing effective stress management strategies. You can write about your practice with the SOLVE Method.

You can find poems and stories that affirm your courage as a single mother. On these pages, feel free to write your own poems or draw scenes that bring the sureness of your courage and visions of the peace you seek.

You can review the strengths you find in your past, and the ones you're using in the present. You might write about the stories of others, and about the teachers whose wisdom and lessons have inspired you to believe in your own resilience and Self-strength.

As you read over what you've written, you'll discover the many ways you've used coping power successfully. In this personal journal you can find the gifts of Soul Mother Wisdom that have inspired you to beat stress before it beats you.

INSIGHT FIVE

Your Psychic Power Unlocks Strength and Wisdom

Wisdom looks like a releasing woman…
with one hand behind her in one great gesture of letting go…
of all the traditions that no longer fit in her hand,
that limit her dance.
Wisdom does not scorn the traditions of yesterday,
she releases them.
Once outside of her grasp, they are free to float to the place
where memories link the best of what was
to all the energies of tomorrow.

AUTHOR UNKNOWN

DESTINATION DESTINY

Driving over dark, curving mountain roads, my mother hunches over the steering wheel. Next to her, in the passenger seat, my father slumps, head on his chest, as we head to "the Doctor's" summer residence. Huddled in back under a blanket of hot tension, my sister and I hope this "Doctor" will somehow restore the playful, upbeat father we love.

I have known for a while that something is wrong. I have seen my father's nervous tics, and once saw him curled up, crying. But now, leaving our beloved mountain vacation in the middle of the night means that what was wrong is worse.

At the cottage, mother disappears as my crumpled father is whisked into a room called "the Office." Settled onto lumpy daybeds on a narrow screened porch on the other side of the Office, Gini and I lie confused and exhausted. Sleepless and in a fog, I attempt to rest. But I am wide awake and startled to witness a scenario not meant for me to see. In the dark quiet night, I struggle to make sense of what is happening on the other side of the screen door.

Directly in my line of vision, sitting on opposite sides of a desk as if in a spotlight, Daddy and the Doctor are speaking silent words. All I hear are crickets chirping a rhythmic score for this latest episode of my father's recurring depressions. This scene now becomes my world, whirling wordless but mystifying questions through my frightened teenage mind.

What is my father saying to the Doctor? What is the Doctor telling him? And what kind of Doctor can possibly understand what is wrong with my father? What can any person say to make another person's misery go away? Will our family be okay? Will *I* be okay?

Eventually the long night ends, and we return to our vacation. My father appears to be okay, but I am changed. I am destined to be scared when I face life's unknowns, and sparked with curiosity for unraveling life's emotional mysteries. That night's barely fathomed questions set in motion my personal missions.

Although years will pass before I will undertake the conscious journey to fulfill these emotional/spiritual inspirations, I have been called to my future—intuitively directed to release the pain of the past, to nurture the emotional wellness of children (especially my own), and to discover the peace and wisdom that breathe in the human Soul.

DESTINATION DESTINY: SCENE TWO

It is another summer. I am climbing the Flume in New Hampshire's White Mountains with my family. After a hospitalization and shock treatments for his depression, my father refers to the hospital, rather than Dartmouth College, as his alma mater. His humor reassures me. If he can joke about something so serious, I assume that he's okay. However, around the next rise of the boardwalk another fright awaits, ready to again carve the course of my life.

As we climb further, my father turns pale. Clutching his chest in fear, he says he cannot breathe. Time stops. Am I about to see my father drop dead on the trail? After frozen minutes he finds his breath, and we go on. But now my fear has made me sharply vigilant of his breathing and his balance. Over and over I ask him urgently, "Are you okay? *Are you okay?*"

Despite reassurances, my fragile safety fragments. It feels as if billions of droplets of security, and Self, float down into the dark rushing waters of the Flume. Now the old question, the real question, destined to haunt me over the years returns.

Will I be okay?

This question will only begin to be answered when, years later, I uncover the power of the psychic dimension, and discover the wisdom to recover the shattered pieces of my Self.

But then, my father survives. Was it altitude sickness, a minor heart event, or possibly a panic attack? We never knew. Until his death from lung cancer years later, he will also survive other episodes of his chronic mental illness, including one severely depressed state in which he will attempt to kill himself.

And how do I survive?

From the Flume forward I am destined to experience severe distress in the face of both actual and perceived danger. I will become overly vigilant to the real or imagined fragility or safety of those I love. When feeling insecure, I will attempt to control circumstances beyond my control. Often I will choose the path that seems safest, including marrying too young rather than facing my truth and jumping into life on my own.

However, there is a plus side. My curiosity to find and fathom the causes and cures for human suffering flares into a passion, and my desire to be less scared and less anxious moves me in two crucial directions. I will pursue and achieve an education in the curative factors and force of social work, and I will become dedicated to discovering the amazing powers of the psychic dimension of mind. The connection between these two paths will inspire me to heal myself as well as help others seek the truth and wisdom of their own authentic Selves.

INTRODUCED TO PSYCHIC POWER

Years later, as terminal cancer is finally about to free my father from his emotional pain, a crucial phase in my journey toward wisdom is about to begin. With two little children, a dying parent, and an unstable marriage, I am about to take a giant step toward my destination. I could say it was unexpected, but I *would* say it was predicted. Here is how it begins.

I have promised my best friend Rita to accompany her to a personal growth program at the local counseling center. However, as the event gets closer, I am not sure. My initial enthusiasm has waned and has been replaced by the usual feelings of fear. At that moment I have absolutely no motivation to enter the world of mental health, about which I know nothing. In fact, the idea terrifies me. I am not the least bit interested in whatever "counseling" means. I am interested only in the cozy safety of my house.

But Rita has other ideas, and to her credit, she is determined. I have promised to go, and we *are* going! Although years later I will thank her for the blessing of her insistence, on that night the fear of losing her friendship becomes greater than the fear of the unknown. Feeling vulnerable and filled with anxiety, I force myself to fulfill my promise. Hours later, rather than being "freaked out" by what I find, I walk into an experience that will begin to answer the long-ago-asked questions, begin to unravel the mysteries, and begin to shape the rest of my life.

To my surprise, the Self-development program fascinates me, and so does the evening's main speaker. Nathan is an intuitive psychic, a minister, and a self-proclaimed healer. His presentation centers on psychic ability and its many applications for healing body and mind. I become immediately intrigued by the possibilities for altering human suffering, and I wonder if the ideas I hear Nathan talking about might help my father in his last days. My curiosity is wildly tweaked and I want to know more!

At the program's close, I introduce myself to Nathan. I tell him about my father's illness, and my embryonic interest in the psychic dimension. As we speak, I feel energy sparkling between us in a way I have never encountered. Incredibly, I have the odd impression that

Nathan and I have known each other before. As I continue speaking with him, I experience what feels like compression of time, as if time seems to shrink—almost not to exist. When our conversation ends, Nathan and I have become long-lost friends.

Whether due to personal temperament, involvement in the family business, or our compromised relationship, Dov is largely unavailable for the type of support that Nathan could, and does, provide. But despite our various differences, Dov is also as fascinated by Nathan's knowledge as I am. Together we welcome Nathan and his wisdom into our lives.

Over the next several weeks, with Dov's blessing, Nathan accompanies me on hospital visits to my father. As we drive he explains the ways in which the psychic dimension of mind can be used for comfort, stress relief, intuitive knowing, and physical/emotional healing. Although I am several years from social work school and single motherhood, Nathan's lessons create foundations for my life's most crucial and beneficial beliefs.

I come to understand that negative emotional states can be altered, that psychic ability can be used to solve problems, and that mind power is a natural form of hypnosis and Self-hypnosis that can create change on levels beyond concrete or overt suggestions. But Nathan also warns me that although we can and may use mind power, only G-d has the final answers.

Nathan's honesty about this basic life truth both scares and reassures me. I want my father to live, but I face the fact that he is very sick and has little time. I am frightened to lose him, but I realize that for the first time in my life I might be able to consciously quiet the anxiety that has been my emotional inheritance.

Though fear races through my mind, my budding understanding of mind power will allow me to find stillness enough to be present for my father's last days, and strength enough to grieve his passing. With Nathan's help and something like courage to bear the loss of my father, I have opened the door to Soul Wisdom, and although I only barely fathom what might come, I intend to walk through.

Soon after my father dies, Nathan offers Dov and me a brief psychic reading for the future. He opens my palm, but quickly and gently closes it. He cannot tell us what he sees, but only that difficulties lie ahead.

Sadly, he tells me that he will not be with me to face what is coming. Nathan's personal path has changed direction, and suddenly he is gone from my life as abruptly as he entered. Although I will never see or hear from Nathan again, all that he has taught me will stay with me, and will fortify me for the arrival of the problems Nathan so accurately predicted.

I have no doubt that Nathan was one of those angels that arrive at exactly the right critical moments and give exactly what they are meant to give. Nathan's short time in my life built the basis of my stress management work, and helped me recognize other teachers as they have appeared. One of these was Ramona Garcia, a talented psychic who taught the "Silva Mind Control" course that Dov and I took at Nathan's urging. Not long after taking Ramona's course, my lessons in the psychic dimension of mind would become a powerful fount of strength and healing during one of my most difficult times.

LESSONS IN THE PSYCHIC DIMENSION

Nathan and Ramona demystified the word "psychic." They taught me that the meaning of "psychic" comes from the Greek word "psyche," which refers to spirit, essence, soul, mind, awareness and consciousness. I learned that we all have the potential to experience the wonders of the psychic dimension and psychic phenomena. Some, like Nathan, Ramona, myself, and most likely some of you, choose to develop, and consciously use, psychic ability.

Ramona and Nathan taught me how to enter the psychic dimension by stilling the mind through relaxation and meditation. Once I could feel what it was like to be at a quiet inner place, I began to understand how the mind can reduce or intensify stress, and how some of the teeniest thoughts that come through may offer some of the most important information.

I was thrilled (and truthfully, a little disappointed) to learn that the psychic power of mind is not magic, but a built-in mental tool that can be used in a variety of everyday ways for beating stress, solving problems, accessing intuitive wisdom, and for deep healing of mind/body/spirit. As I continued to discover more about the way the psychic dimension and the power of mind overlap and interact, my lessons became more interesting.

I learned about two main types of psychic ability: receptive and projective. Receptive psychic intuition is often spontaneous, but can also be applied intentionally using the same techniques for stilling the mind and opening to information that are similar to the steps of the SOLVE Method.

As it turns out, the way to engage the receptive psychic power of mind is to relax, pay attention to what comes in, and evaluate the information in relation to your situation. Receptive psychic ability can assist in problem solving and can help to lower stress.

Projective psychic ability is fascinating and potentially very useful. It involves conscious intention to use mental imagery and suggestion for any positive purpose (emphasis on "positive"), such as transmitting healing to another person or situation. The uses of projective psychic energy for stress relief or health improvement have been mainstreamed by practitioners of Reiki and Therapeutic Touch, techniques which are actually used in many hospitals today as adjuncts to traditional medical healing.

Some use projective energy in prayer or healing circle meditations. For example, in my stress management groups we often create a "healing circle" in which we send healing to another person, place or situation. Often the feedback is amazing, such as the time we "worked on" a person who had been diagnosed with cancer behind his eye. We were informed a few weeks later that the tumor was gone! Did our projections make a difference? We never knew for sure, but we had our beliefs!

Whether using receptive psychic intuition to receive or projective psychic intuition to send, or using the two bands of psychic intuition simultaneously, Ramona cautioned to direct the mind away from distorted thinking that creates false beliefs, or falsely believing that you can make bad things happen to yourself or others. She taught us that receptive and projective psychic functioning are about wisdom, strength and healing. False and negative beliefs limit authentic psychic potential.

Ramona taught us two positive affirmations to use for clearing a positive and authentic channel to the psychic dimension. I use these to center myself in preparation for both psychic and clinical work. These affirmations are powerful stress reducers. You can incorporate them into your stress management tool kit.

Negative thoughts will have no ill effect on me or anyone else.

All forces in the universe are now working toward my higher good, and the good of all concerned.

Underlying these affirmations, and others like them, are key beliefs that emphasize the following:

You have no power to make bad things happen.
You have the power to achieve mental peace and increase the well-being of yourself and your children.
You did not cause and cannot cause bad things to happen because you had a bad thought.
No matter how hard you try, you cannot control everything—even with psychic ability.
The final "say" is out of our hands, and in the end is in the hands of a Higher Power of your personal understanding.

My teachers also made it clear that although the word "psychic" sometimes carries a tinge of fakery, the psychic skills of clairvoyance, precognition, creativity, imagination, and intuition are real and valuable assets of the psychic dimension of mind. In fact, they are intricately related to the inner voice of authentic Self and the wisdom of the Soul.

In her book *Women Who Run With the Wolves*, Clarissa Pinkola Estes explains the psychic dimension, or the wise dimension, of the mind like this:

Ancient dissectionists spoke of the auditory nerve being divided into three or more pathways deep in the brain. They surmised that the ear was meant...to hear at three different levels. One pathway was said to hear the mundane conversations of the world. A second pathway apprehended learning and art. And a third pathway existed so the soul itself might hear guidance and gain knowledge while here on earth.

Now, if you are ready, you might like to have an experience with psychic projection and reception. Remember the Lemon Effect? The way of the psychic dimension is not usually—or unusually—particularly dramatic, but often as simple as thinking of a lemon. Imagery for healing body or mind works the same way that the imagined sense of seeing, feeling, cutting, and tasting a lemon can prime the salivary glands. Psychic/intuitive information can be as ordinary as imagining the taste of your favorite food. For example, the following experience qualifies as psychic because it happens at the inner dimension of your mind.

As you settle into a comfortable spot, take a gentle, easy breath. As you relax, you can use mental creativity to project your imagination to a place you know and like, a new place you would like to visit, or an imaginary place that you create in your mind.

Take a few moments to use sense imagery to receive a felt sense of truly being in your place. You can use all your senses.

See the variety of sights.

Smell the air, the flowers, the food.

Go out to eat, have a picnic.

Hear the sounds. Go to a concert, listen to a bird.

You can even allow yourself a tactile experience like touching fabrics or cutting flowers.

You can also seek to receive wisdom while on this psychic visit. If you wish, invite a friend—real or imaginary—to join you. Your "friend" can offer wise counsel or insights and information for creative ideas and solutions for current problems.

Take a few moments to be with the person or people who are there to assist and inspire you. Just notice what you think and how you feel. When you are ready, gently begin your return to the outer dimension.

In reorienting, you can affirm that you will come back refreshed, revitalized, and peaceful, able to continue to use experiences like this to help you be more creative, more peaceful, to manage stress more effectively, and to open clear channels to Soul Mother Wisdom.

As you practice and become more aware of the power of receptive and projective psychic "knowing," you might notice that your trust in the connection to your intuitive part is increasing. You may become aware that you can request and receive information through the wise inner voice of your Soul.

PSYCHIC KNOWING–PROOF ENOUGH FOR ME

One colorful October day shortly after my father died I had an experience that proved for me beyond a doubt that psychic knowing is real and that it works.

Picture this: The girls and I are driving to meet a friend and her children for a picnic. I feel peaceful, but suddenly, out of the blue, I am taken aback as the image of a hospital room emerges uninvited into my mind. Because Nathan and Ramona have taught me that such experiences can reveal wisdom, I allow this vision to unfold, preparing myself to see a flashback of my father's last days. But I am totally unprepared for what I see—and for what, unbelievably, I understand.

I see myself in some hospital room, walking toward a closed curtain. I know that behind the curtain will be a bed. Slowly and quickly the image evolves as if directed outside of myself. I approach the curtain, and also watch myself approaching the bed. I remain in the dual dimensions of doer and observer as I part the curtain. Now the image pans, like a movie camera, to a closeup of the patient. I recognize the face immediately. The patient in the bed is not my father. To my shock, the patient is clearly and unmistakably my husband!

Frightened, I force the disturbing image from my mind, convincing myself it is only a scary daydream. I determine to pay closer attention to driving, but all I have learned about intuition remains in my mind. Later, I will discover that clairvoyance and precognition have become part of my newly found psychic abilities.

Arriving home, I notice a familiar yellow convertible parked at our house. Stress and fear rocket. My mother-in-law doesn't drop in, especially when I'm out. Something is wrong, and incredibly, I know what it is!

Dov's mother's first words wash over me. I am barely able to hear, think, or even breathe. But her face tells me what I already know. I manage to say, "I know. Dov's had a heart attack."

With pain in her eyes, she asks, "How did you know?"

"I just did," I reply. "I just did."

How can I tell her about the afternoon's premonition or others that I've been receiving—like dreaming that my chest is being crushed, or having the troubling feeling that Dov is going to die before he's forty?

(Which, in fact, he does.) How could I reveal that I've been confiding my fear to Ramona, who has been counseling me to use the psychic power of mind to project and to hold the image of Dov alive and well? My in-laws are traditional, down-to-earth people. I would sound like a kook. (Maybe I *am* a kook!) But it doesn't matter, for whatever has been intuited is real, and I must cope with what it means for my life.

Dov is thirty. Our oldest daughter is four, and the baby is fifteen months. I don't even know if Dov will live. All I know is that one way or another, I must deal. I have a dim hope that mind power will help me—but how?

The first clue comes from Ramona.

"Dov's had a heart attack!" I announce to her, stumbling over the words. *"But why?"* I ask. "I've been using all the projective techniques you taught me! Shouldn't that have prevented it?"

"Kitten," Ramona assures me in her soft, caring way. "Instead of falling on concrete, he fell on a feather bed. Don't you see? The mind strategies have worked!"

Because of my stress I had been unable to see that perhaps my projecting had been successful in some way. Ramona suggested that I continue to use projective psychic power by writing scripts that then we called "programs." She directed me to read them to Dov.

These "programs" would tell Dov's heart that it had no disease or disharmonies. With the understanding we have today about the mind/body connection, we can recognize that what we called "programs" are actually a form of hypnosis that could mobilize Dov's unconscious mind for healing and reduce his stress, which could also promote healing.

But in those medieval days of the seventies and early eighties, holistic ideas were hocus-pocus, on the medical fringe. Nevertheless, amazed by my premonitions and buoyed by my trust in Ramona, I was willing to give mind power another serious try.

But first I needed permission from the doctor to read the "programs" to Dov. "Well, I can't see how this stuff could hurt" served as medical sanction, and with that I went to work reading to Dov the programs I created. When not directly reading I sent healing via visualization by picturing Dov's heart on a mental blackboard and erasing imagined damage.

Ramona gave me three key ideas for sending psychic healing to Dov with projective mind power and trusting that his mind power, whether or not he was aware of it at the time, would receive the healing. These ideas were:

- **Picture Dov healthy now.** Use "is healthy" as opposed to "will be" healthy. Believe this as if it is now.
- **Use images** to increase the psychic impact, the power. Imagine them as if on a mental movie screen. The anatomical specifics in the imagery are not crucial. Images can be realistic or imaginary. It's the power of intention that's important. Trust that Dov's receptive ability will receive the sent images and take them "to heart."
- **Use metaphors** to image and project healing, ramping up the psychic power of the projections.

Although I continued to project healing to Dov in person or at a distance for the month he was in the hospital—it was just before the dawning of a new understanding of heart health as well as of psychic understanding—it took only a few days to find out how powerful the psychic mind could be. Originally, Dov's cardiologist had told us that Dov's EKG showed a "bubble" in the heart wall. However, after a few days of "programming," the same doctor greeted us excitedly. The doctor was flabbergasted, and his report was astounding. He told us that the bubble was completely gone! It had not shown up on a subsequent EKG!

Not one of Dov's doctors, including heart specialists, could offer a medical reason for the bubble's disappearance. Every one of them had come to the conclusion that they had read the electrocardiogram wrong! I leave it to you to draw your own conclusions.

While we will never positively know the reason for the disappearance of the bubble, we now do know that using positive images and affirmations, as I did with Dov, can constitute a powerful way to promote health and healing. As I mentioned before, mind power in the form of Therapeutic Touch or Reiki are now considered viable and acceptable assets for enhancing patients' outcomes. Mind-powered affirmation "programs" and exercises are also often used to prepare patients for surgery.

However, rest assured that you do not have to be ill to hasten positive results of your actions, or derive other beneficial effects of psychic mind power. Using affirmations, programs and scripts can constitute a powerful tool for single mothers to reduce their stress, provide an energy boost and enhance coping strength.

Today, health-affirming programs can be found in many daily inspirational books and on the worldwide web. Of course, you can also write your own programs to fit your personal needs. Just remember to state your desired outcome as if it already is.

Following is an example of a program that uses projective power for sending healing and receptive power for believing in it. You might use a program like this for general health. As you read, breathe naturally and notice what you experience.

As you settle into a deeply relaxed state, imagine being surrounded by a brilliant healing light. You can perceive this light in any color, shape, size or intensity that you can imagine.

Now, gently and softly, imagine that the healing energy of this light permeates your body and mind, restoring and rejuvenating every level of your being—physical, emotional, mental, and spiritual.

As you feel the healing energy surround you, imagine it increasing, filling you, covering you, and comforting you with its power. Affirm that disharmony anywhere in your body, mind, or emotions is now being neutralized and discharged. Feel the soothing relief of stress being released as you let go.

You are now in perfect balance. Your body is in perfect health. Every day, in every way you are getting better, better, and better.

And as Ramona always would add, "And this is so!"

A Preview of Single Motherhood and More Psychic Lessons

You will not be surprised to learn that Dov's quick rebound amazed everyone. So impressed was the hospital that a subsequent newsletter featured his story—minus the use of psychic healing, of course! But these were different times. After discharge, Dov's doctors ordered bed rest for many more weeks, with the additional Rx of absolutely no stress.

No problem—I had stress enough for two! I believed Dov's life and our survival was my responsibility. Expecting little or nothing from Dov, I assumed full parenting and family management. I cooked heart-healthy meals, tended the kids, arranged play dates and medical appointments, and ran interference with friends and relatives. I pledged to keep the little ones from "stressing" daddy, lest he drop dead. (Fortunately, I had enough wisdom not to frighten them with that!) I was running the show pretty much alone, deeply afraid of the possibility of ever having to run the show alone for "real."

I labored under the illusion that by controlling everything—including what I could not control—I could ward off disaster. But as my fatigue and stress went up, my connection with my inner psychic wisdom—my only true control—went down. As I was drowning in fear, the life raft offered by mind power was floating temporarily beyond my reach.

Yet even so, in the still-operational psychic power of my mind I sensed a distant truth. I felt that somehow I was being prepared for a different time, a time coming when true "control" would be conscious awareness of choosing my responses to major life stressors.

I sensed a time coming when marital separation, a painful divorce, the demands and rewards of social work school, the death of my former husband, and the responsibility of single motherhood would lead back to the most passionate motivations of my life—the fervent wish to be okay, to be the most successful parent (and person) I could be, and to teach others, especially single mothers, how to thrive and succeed with positive mental health and the psychic gifts of the mind.

During my exquisitely inspired time with Nathan, he had taught me how to use intuition to actually do psychic readings. Later, through Ramona's courses and through private sessions with her, Ramona helped me refine this aspect of psychic skill, and encouraged me that I had ability to do readings professionally. Because I had entered social work school around the same time that my marriage ended, my funds were scarce, and I found I could augment my monthly support from Dov by working at psychic fairs on the weekends when the girls were with him. It was during this time that I met Herb Dewey, an accomplished Tarot card reader and an acclaimed psychic.

Herb became my third psychic teacher. He taught me how to stop second-guessing my intuition, how to trust and follow my impressions, and how to interpret what I saw, sensed or felt. Herb explained how to not scare people, but to use compassion and empathy in presenting readings. He taught me how to keep mental boundaries in order to distinguish what issues were mine and which ones belonged to the other person.

Herb emphasized that as readers, we were merely vehicles for receiving and offering information to the "client" in the gentlest and most useful way. Prophets we were not! Were we going to make dead people materialize? No! And neither were we going to let others think we could direct their lives. We were to refrain from telling people what to do, but rather practice using our skills to empower others and help them believe in their own inner wisdom.

This ethical schema, as it turned out, was consistent with the professional standards of social work, including the emphasis on Self-determination. Fulfilling these standards and ethics required that I attend to my own personal growth. From my initial fears of counseling and psychology I had come far. Now I devoted myself to the development of my solid, authentic Self, and to the service of the mental/emotional health of others.

I remained dedicated to my social work education, to the highest ethical standards of my psychic work, and to the health and well-being of my daughters. As I continued to increase my understanding of mind power, it became clear that there is wisdom available at the psychic dimension that might be immensely helpful in bringing about balanced thinking, effective coping, and successful stress management. Could it be possible for me to use the power of mind to fulfill these goals and access my strength and resilience?

Nathan, Ramona, and Herb helped open me to the gift of psychic wisdom, and my social work education was giving me clinical principles by which to understand what it meant to have a strong and solid Self as a woman and as a mother. I was continuing to unravel and understand the causes of human misery and the role of the wise inner voice for achieving correction. The benefits of mental clarity, intuitive wisdom, and emotional balance were becoming my guiding lights and shining a beacon of hope for my life as a single mother.

THE PSYCHIC POWER IN YOUR SINGLE MOTHER STORY

This might be just the right time to think about the various chapters of your own story. Such reflection can show you occasions when you might have become aware of or experienced the psychic power of mind. Perhaps you will remember a time when you were intuitively impressed with a correct solution to a problem, or think of a time when your intuition helped you release some painful or negative belief held over from your past. You might recognize a time when your Soul Wisdom guided you to change your thinking in order to reduce your stress or improve your health.

You might think back and remember who has come into your life to teach you about wisdom. Perhaps there are such teachers in your life right now. Occasionally teachers are as recognizable as Nathan and Ramona. Sometimes they are more subtle, recognized only later through the wisdom of the psychic dimension.

You can also take a psychic look into the present. What problems do you now have that might be solved by stilling your mind and receiving psychic information? Are there problems that could be helped via the projective power of the mind?

What you discover in your story can affirm the existence of the psychic dimension of mind, and reassure you that you have the ability to use its power. With psychic power you can heal your stress, succeed in adding positive meaning to your story, and transform confusion into wisdom. You can change anxiety into peace, and become more authentically who you truly are.

TIPS FOR UNDERSTANDING PSYCHIC POWER

- Look for the ordinary and simple in the psychic realm. Psychic power does not necessarily—or always—have to do with clairvoyance—seeing things before they happen—or clairsentience—sensing information that is unknown or partially known. Psychic power can be as simple as being impressed to change a negative thought into a positive, or intuitively sensing the correct action to take in a problematic situation. You are "psychic" when you have a hunch that someone is about to call, intuit a new solution to an old problem, or discover a wise new meaning for an important part of your story.

- Notice the way mind power overlaps with effective stress management and quality mental health in what is called the mind/body connection, or "the mind/body/spirit connection." If the Lemon Experiment and the vanished heart bubble reassured you that your mind is powerful and can affect what you experience, you can better understand how quieting the mind can open the spiritual channel to wisdom and become a major factor in achieving health—mental, physical, and spiritual.

- Believe that what you tell yourself matters, because it does. Are you saying that you are "dying for a cigarette?" Is someone a "pain in the neck?" (Or somewhere else?) Have you told someone to "get off my back?"

Many years ago I had a patient who had a sick husband. Over and over she kept saying, "I can't stand it!" I "read" this on an intuitive level, and suggested she might want to take care of some problems she might be having with her feet.

"How did you know?" she asked.

"You were telling yourself that you could not stand!" I reflected back.

She understood and was motivated, which enabled a discussion of the ways she could rephrase her wording to promote the healing of her feet.

- Remember that you can have an effect on your body and your mind, but you cannot make bad things happen. You can use positive affirmations suggested by Ramona and others. You can also write your own. Positive suggestions and programs have the power to keep you out of the world of guilt, worry, and stress and land you in the world of healing, serenity, and wisdom.

- Envision a felt sense of the issues as if they have been already resolved, even if you don't know exactly how to resolve them. Just holding the positive vision can relieve stress, lead to solutions, and unlock strength and wisdom.

Ideas for Reflection and Insight:
Use Metaphor to Change Your Vision
(of Your Life and Your Self)

Metaphors are images that describe something by comparing it symbolically to something else. You can use metaphors to psychically change your perception of your Self and the way you envision your single mother life. Using metaphors at the inner dimension of the mind has the power to shift your emotions and improve your sense of your Self as a parent, and as a person.

Following is an example of the psychic power of metaphor to bring about Soul Mother Wisdom:

A single mother named Glenda described herself to me as "a piece of litter, tossed aside by a rejecting partner and many disappointing subsequent relationships." She worried that her negative sense of Self would adversely affect her children, but her desire for their well-being motivated Glenda to change herself.

Glenda also told me that she had "landed on her feet" in many difficult situations. I suggested to Glenda that she allow the "litter" to float away and bring to mind an image that represented the positive ways she had coped after her "landings."

As Glenda proceeded, she was intuitively impressed with the image of a lithe and limber panther, charging with determination and landing softly on powerful feet to conquer its prey.

Using the metaphor of the "prey" to describe her stressors and the metaphor of the panther to describe her quiet yet strong determination to prevail, Glenda was inspired to stop seeing herself as flotsam buffeted about by forces beyond her control, but rather to vision herself as a strong, determined mother panther. Seeing herself this way changed Glenda's Self image, created awareness of her courage, and brought about a deep compassion for her Self-strength.

If you would like to create a new metaphor for your Self, you can use the following exercise. Notice the differences in your sensations, emotions, body postures, and your state of mind as you proceed.

Take a moment to bring to mind adjectives you typically use to describe your Self. If you find negatives, you can release them.

When you find positive descriptors, imagine symbols that represent these qualities. The symbols can be anything that comes to mind—an animal, something of nature, an inanimate object, a line or phrase from a song, or a scene from a movie. Accept your images as metaphors, psychically symbolizing your positive qualities. If negative thoughts come in, just let them come and go.

Memorize your new mental images and the feelings, thoughts, and sensations associated with them.

As you go forward into your life, whenever negative descriptors or sour emotions come to mind, consciously bring forward new metaphors for your Self. The mind/body/spirit connection will do its work, intuitively reminding you of the truth of your authentic Self and clearing psychic space for the emergence of Soul Mother Wisdom.

PAGES FOR JOURNALING

You do not have to give up smoking, love everyone, or never get annoyed, but you can change how you talk to yourself and how you think. The use of psychic ability to change your state of mind, and/or your emotional state, takes some practice. However, being mindful of your internal conversation with your Self (even if you're imagining a conversation with someone else!) and willingness to use the positive power of mind can move you closer to a destination of wholeness, and to the solid *felt sense* of Soul Mother Wisdom.

On these pages you can journal about your Self-talk. You can write healing scripts and life-changing programs. And you can create new metaphors. You can come back and visit, read and reflect on the changes you have made and the areas in which you wish to change.

You might find it helpful to write about times when you used the psychic power of mind for healing, problem solving, and parenting success. The more you can unlock the resources of wisdom within the psychic dimension of Self, the more you can release the negative emotional traditions of yesterday and enrich your single mother life of today.

INSIGHT SIX

Soul Wisdom Empowers Your Parenting

"One of the greatest gifts a mother can give her children is to clarify her own life goals, develop her own maturity, and fulfill her potential for creating a satisfying life for herself and her children. Her courage and her success will be a legacy for her children and her grandchildren."

SINGLE MOTHER, CIRCA 2005

EMPOWERED PARENTING

Single mothers travel a particularly challenging road. While it's hard enough for two parents to supply all that children need for healthy development, as a single mother managing never-ending demands that try your patience and test your endurance, you need a set of practical strategies, a solid sense of Self, and a Soul connection to your mother's intuition.

With the powerful combination of Self, Soul, and a few good strategies you will have the know-how, confidence, and insight to balance the requirements of daily life with the best interests of your children and your own Self-care. You will understand dilemmas, handle problems, and navigate obstacles with power steering, and parent from mental clarity rather than from fear, guilt, or resentment. With practice, you will live life with less stress and more peace.

If that all sounds good, it's because it is! Parenting experts agree that when mothers operate from a solid core of authentic Self and a rich supply of wisdom, their children have a better chance of developing into well-adjusted adults. When Meta-maturity, Responsive-resilience and Self-strength (true MRS) guide your path, and you utilize the insights of psychic intuition to navigate the road, Soul Mother Wisdom will empower your parenting. By reflecting on situations from daily life, you can discover examples of the way in which your parenting has been empowered by wisdom.

Below are some situations typical of ones you may have experienced. As you read and reflect, you can begin to see the ways in which wisdom, whether consciously received or automatically understood, is involved in the practical and usual details of single mother life. Notice the resilience, Self-strength, and parenting wisdom in each example. As you read, you can come to realize your own wisdom. If you realize skills you want to work on, good for you! Growth is a gift to yourself and your children.

REFLECTIONS

Perhaps there was a time when, even though you were pressured, you took time to soothe your frightened child. Because you understood her needs and how your support could benefit her, you took time to help. You understood that by helping her learn to manage stress in the present, you reduced the potential for similar stress in the future.

Perhaps you used Soul Mother Wisdom when you chose to make one more tired trip up the stairs or down the hall to comfort an upset child. Perhaps you preferred to yell, "I'm too tired, and I am not coming! So go to sleep!" However, your connection to your true MRS may have advised that tending to an existing problem might avert larger ones. Perhaps you understood that gently soothing a crying child could help him learn to soothe himself, and get you to bed a bit sooner.

Once you know your child is settled and all is well, perhaps your inner wisdom advises you that a firm and kind approach can work best. In those situations you understand that it makes sense to gently set a limit on the number of trips you're willing to make. When you realize that children need attention *and* limits and you understand that it's okay to balance their needs with your own, Soul Mother Wisdom is serving you well!

Perhaps on a day when you had a lot of work to do, or just wanted to veg out, you decided instead to spend a few minutes playing with your little boy, or talking to him about his school day. Your true MRS advised that spending some quality minutes with your son might be more productive than pushing him away. You knew intuitively and strategically that a little attention feeds your child's self-esteem like a miracle fertilizer.

Soul Mother parenting wisdom can come in many different ways. Does it come to you in the silent moment when you take a breath and realize what you need to do to resolve a difficult dilemma? Does it feel like freedom from inner conflict when you know the right action to take—even though you *really* want to do the other thing?

It can be helpful to notice the way in which parenting wisdom presents itself to you. Notice the thoughts and feelings that seem to come from emotional pain, and those that seem to emerge from a wiser part of your Self. While at times all single mothers experience sadness, anger, fear, or other leftovers of old hurts, you now know that when you want to you can shift into intuitive knowing. By practicing the shift, you will be able to parent more frequently with the insights and confidence of Soul Mother Wisdom.

The following affirmation can help you shift into wisdom:

With the clarity and security of my solid Self, I enter the dimension of Soul Mother Wisdom. Now wise intuition informs my parenting, and inspires all my situations. I realize positive Self-messages that uplift and comfort me. I place trust in my authentic Self, which knows. From the vantage point of Soul Mother Wisdom I envision all that has prepared me for my mission. I see the vista of my story, and all the ways in which I have had courage and have hope. I trust that I am able to see what is best for my children and for myself. I am doing my best, and my best is good enough.

SINGLE MOTHERS COMMENT:
WISDOM IN ACTION

There are virtually endless examples of Soul Mother Wisdom shaping the insights and effectiveness of single parenting. When you recognize wisdom in the parenting choices of others, you can better realize the way Soul Mother Wisdom can empower your own. The wisdom to make effective parenting choices can mean healthy growth for your children, relief for your stress, and progress on your path to inner peace.

"Single motherhood is not a terminal illness. You can get beyond it. If you're divorced, you go through a grief process. You can forgive. I have four kids. Not only am I raising them alone, but I am also home schooling them. There's a lot of stress connected with that. Crisis and chaos can disturb your peace of mind. Kids and all their needs can tend to disrupt clear thinking. But prayer has helped me to refocus problems. That gives me a clearer sense of purpose and direction. I pray every day for my children and for others."

"My friend has it hard. I'm lucky. I have a safety net—family and friends. She doesn't have that, and it's made things harder for her. Her son doesn't want to be away from her, and she's not well. If she needs hospitalization, she doesn't know what she'll do. She told me she's thought about driving into the back of a truck. I went to her therapist with her, and we agreed that I would be part of her safety plan. She says no one has ever been there for her. I have some idea of what she's going through because there are times when I really feel alone. My friend has to learn to be there for herself. I've had to learn to be there for myself."

"My hope got used up. But sometimes hope is a head idea. True hope is in the heart. I know things will get better for me and my kids. I have this certain feeling that I can rebuild a dream and believe in hope again."

"I was a single mother in a marriage. I could not emotionally or mentally afford to keep him (alcoholic husband) any more. It was survival. I would have had to drag him around, and he'd be the cause of our losing everything. I couldn't give any more, and I couldn't take his behavior anymore, but he was still in the house. When he was in the house, I could get a little break—with him gone, there would be no break. But I needed to really let go. Finally I had an intuitive moment when I knew I had to be completely on my own and build a foundation for a new life. With him gone there was relief, and I can live for me and my child. I pray every day for the tenacity to keep it all going."

"I was blindsided by the end of my marriage. I was full of fear and shame. I felt tumult and rage. My life was in chaos. I was trying to cope with change, deal with reactions of my family, and support my kids—and not go crazy. But I would have moments of deep knowing. Then I knew that for the sake of my children I had to move, and accept that my ex had a new life. But a still small voice said to not cut off from my children's father or his new wife. The still small voice told me that cutting off was not going to be part of my story."

"When all this happened to me I was under a 'spell,' still believing that what I was outside was more important than who I was inside. Then I came to the realization that I had to accept what is. I had to trust myself, love myself, and honor all my parts to do what I had to do for my children and myself."

"I'm so afraid that the task is too overwhelming and that I will be stuck and resent this poor little baby for taking over my life. What if I didn't take good care of the baby? I don't want to be like my friend who doesn't seem to really care about her baby and resents everything the kid is about. So I went to a single-mothers-by-choice meeting, and it was good to see women in all different stages. They all said it's the most difficult thing and the most wonderful thing. I wouldn't give it up for anything."

"Prayer helps me step back from problems…and get guidance about decisions and steps I have to take for our life. I also stay open to what I read or hear, and sometimes I get a clear impression in my mind. When God speaks to me it is not in an audible voice, but a strong sense of something that might jump out at me."

URSULA'S STORY: A PATH TO STRENGTH AND PEACE

One of the most poignant examples of parenting with Soul Mother Wisdom can be found in Ursula's story. As you read, notice the moment when Ursula's maturity gives her the wisdom to make choices in the best interest of her children and her Self. You might ask yourself what might you have done in Ursula's situation?

"Devastated!" This was Ursula's reaction to her husband's sudden and tragic death. After several unsuccessful attempts at sobriety, Charles drove his car into a tree, leaving Ursula to raise their two daughters.

Ursula described her initial inability to function, and recollected the moment her wisdom kicked in.

"At first I cried for days. I was consumed with misery, unable to function, and unaware of what my girls needed. My best friend did everything—cooked, cleaned, and got me up to eat. I tried to feel better, but nothing worked. Charles' accident cost me my identity. I was no longer a Mrs.

"Then one day when I couldn't stand my own suffering anymore I picked up a brass bell and smashed it to the floor. My daughter saw me do it. Horrified and frightened, she screamed at me. 'What about us? *What about us?*'"

Ursula calls this event a pivotal moment in her single motherhood. Her daughter's outburst shook Ursula into the realization that she'd been so lost in grief that she'd been oblivious to her children's needs. With this awareness Ursula shifted her mindset. Now her priority became "Giving my girls the childhood they deserved, and making sure they would be okay." With this wise insight guiding her parenting, Ursula made some changes.

Ursula pledged that, to the best of her human ability, she would stay aware of her children's needs. She would refrain from using them as a sounding board for her sadness—or, as she puts it, "for anything to kick a ball against." Instead, she would seek adult support for venting her sadness. Realizing that her girls "just needed me to be there," Ursula became more involved in doing interesting and affordable activities with her children. Although they took some golf lessons and went ice-skating together, as Ursula told me it was not the "thing" they did that mattered—it was being together, even just hanging out, that was important.

In this process Ursula discovered that, regardless of the activity, after at least twenty minutes together her daughters would "open up" and reveal how they were recovering from the loss of their father. Ursula now understood that how she was coping had an effect on her children, and that wise parenting could bring about new relationships with them. Ursula advises single moms, "Be patient, be present, and they will open up to you."

But Ursula also did need to deal with her own healing. "To be aware of how the kids were doing and what they needed, I needed to transcend my own pain," she told me. Committed to quality single parenting—to parenting, period!—Ursula pledged to give her children "a mother they could be proud of."

Toward this goal, Ursula continued to develop her maturity, resilience, and strength. She went into therapy, began an exercise program, went to work for a doctor as a medical aesthetician, and took personal inventory of her own sobriety. Working toward having a solid Self and being the best mother she could be has proven to be a path to healing and becoming wise for Ursula, and a path to success for her and her children.

Now that Ursula's girls are pursuing lives and careers of their own, Ursula feels satisfied that she was able to bring up her children well and create a fulfilling life for herself. Today she pursues a realm of personal interests, has a support network of friends, and owns and operates a successful skin salon. Ursula acknowledges that although the day-to-day life of a single mother is not an easy one, it was important to her to be the person *she* could be proud of. Ursula affirms, "I am a much better person. Single motherhood has been my path to strength and healing."

When I asked Ursula what parenting and healing suggestions she would recommend for other single mothers, she offered these thoughts for you to consider.

URSULA'S TIPS FOR SINGLE MOTHERS

Get Support.

Although it was sometimes painful to hear or read other single mothers' stories, Ursula says she craved stories of strength and courage in order to get beyond her own pain. She needed the support of knowing that she was not alone. She recommends that single mothers seek one another, and share the experiences, strengths, and hope in their stories.

Exercise.

Ursula believes that her exercise program helped her rule out substances for comfort. "Drugs and alcohol are not the answer," she says. Ursula encourages single mothers to focus on healthier ways, such as rest, a healthy diet, exercise, and peer and professional support, to relieve stress and painful emotions.

Be Your True Self.

Although part of her would have liked to recreate the "intact family" as soon as possible, Ursula intuitively knew that what she really needed was the maturity, resilience, and strength to parent effectively and be emotionally ready for another partnership when the time was right. "How could I know someone else, if I did not know myself?"

Trust Your Ability to Grow.

Although she can relapse into pain when certain events remind her of her loss, Ursula trusts her intention and her ability to grow. She believes that when you are focused on knowing your Self, even the painful events can be gifts to yourself and your children.

Adjust Your Mindset.

It would have been easy to harp on "poor me," Ursula admits. However, deciding to make the children the priority without giving up on her Self is Ursula's most important advice. "I wouldn't be who I am if this had not happened," she told me. "I was in a warm, comfortable bubble, and I didn't know life. When the bubble burst, I didn't know who I was anymore. It was a huge blow to my system, but it was a rebirth. My kids have made me better." Ursula concludes, "There was a gift in the problem. There always is."

Perhaps this a good time to continue reflecting on experiences from your own life that have revealed the ways Soul Mother Wisdom has influenced your thinking, emotions, and actions. You might try the following exercise to get into an insightful frame of mind.

> Start with a couple of gentle, easy breaths. As you begin to feel comfortable, you can settle into a peaceful place that is uniquely suited to you. Now you can allow yourself to be in harmony with your body, and with your special way of being at ease in your own inner consciousness. As you become mindful of what you are thinking and feeling, you can begin to notice the way in which insights emerge into awareness.
>
> As you remain still and peaceful you can begin to feel the spirit of light and insight moving easily through your body, infusing your mind and body with life-giving energy. As energy moves

through you, you can affirm for yourself that whatever insights and healing you need at this time, or any other time, will come to you effortlessly.

Now you can bring to mind situations past or current in which your decisions and actions have flowed from Meta-maturity, Responsive-resilience, and Self-strength. You can realize the ways in which have you accessed and utilized these qualities, and the ways in which these qualities, and the ways in which they have influenced your parenting.

When you are ready, your wise Self can anchor confidence into your belief system that you have the strengths of MRS and the guidance of Soul Mother Wisdom, and that you know how to parent with skill and with the serenity that you and your children deserve. Affirm that you can continue to derive what you desire and need from your connection to your intuitive Self.

You can now choose to stay in this reflective dimension for a while longer, returning to your reading later. Or you can choose to stay immersed in inner peace as you open your eyes to continue your reading.

PARENTING WITH SOUL WISDOM

Living life as a single mother can test your courage, tug your heartstrings, and teach you to parent with Soul Wisdom. Although some experiences may cast you into unknown territory, as both Dov's first heart attack and his death did me, others may present a preview of a life lesson you may need to learn. Sometimes seemingly ordinary circumstances can spark a deeper understanding of your authentic Self.

As we cope with life events, Soul Wisdom can continue to supply rich creative benefits for you and your children. The ways in which you recognize, understand, and apply your wisdom will be unique to you and to the meaning you incorporate into your life story. The more you parent with wisdom, the more potential you will have for raising healthy kids with attitudes and behaviors that have potential for success.

My own life reveals the unfolding nature of Soul Wisdom. For example, when my marriage ended, the life I knew ended, too. In my grief and fear I wasn't sure I could live a satisfying life, let alone live one as a single parent. Fortunately Katy's lessons, the wisdom of my savvy therapist, and my own conscious efforts taught me that no one, even Dov, was the single source of my well-being.

With a bit of time, some useful parenting ideas, and the development of Soul Wisdom, the truth unfolded. I discovered that I did have enough resilience and courage to rebuild a good life for myself and my children. As my daughters grew, and as my MRS grew, I found that Soul Wisdom also grows and continues to offer insights and guidance to help manage the changing needs of children as they get older and become adults.

One particular chapter of my story illustrates how parenting older and adult children can bring new and surprising dimensions of meaning to your life story, and reveals the way in which understanding new aspects of the parent/child relationships can deepen the insights of Soul Wisdom. For me, this happened when my firstborn became a wife.

After their father died, my daughters and I bonded into a tight unit. I didn't see us as "us against the world," but rather saw the three of us as "just us," a small, but real, family. This was a good thing, a new positive identification as a family unit. As I settled into our three-ness, I formed the comforting feeling of "forever." As a result, during the girls' growing up years I did not anticipate or even think about a time when my precious threesome would change. When daughter number one got married, that time arrived.

While the walk down the aisle felt only a little bit like walking the last mile, the experience of "giving away" my child surprised me with feelings of loss that I thought I'd already mastered. As for coping with change—I had thought I was good to go! "If I could survive the emotional storms of separation, divorce, and the death of their father," I told myself, "why am I having all these feelings now?"

I was blindsided. I had never thought about "giving away" my children. Hadn't they become *all mine* after their father died? I was unprepared for the onslaught of emotions and questions that came with this new phase. "Will I lose her?" "What will life be like now?" "Did I *really* give her away—or horrors!—give her up?" What happens next?"

I was more confused than I'd been in a long time, but as often is the case with Soul Wisdom, insights came unexpectedly a few weeks later. This time, during a trip to a major therapy conference.

At that year's Evolution of Psychotherapy Conference I heard the "experts" in virtually all realms of family psychotherapy speak about their own issues and frailties. Their wisdom, savvy, and honesty brought me to new levels of understanding of my Self, and the new phase of single motherhood which I had just entered.

As I listened to the speakers teach about life and emotions, I reflected on my own. I flashed back to an earlier time in my story when my babies were born. I could remember what it felt like to hold them and feel the sensation of my heart being awakened to a new kind of love. Sitting in the workshops, I re-experienced these feelings in full emotional color.

As the memory progressed, I remembered how hard it had been to raise my girls after my divorce, and particularly after their father died. I remembered the times I wanted to tell them how hard it was to be a single mother, and how hard it was to resist the temptation to tell. Maybe they knew. Maybe they didn't. I didn't know. I still don't. I do know all the ways I strove to bring them into womanhood without the contamination of my own disappointments, hurts, and negative feelings.

In one particularly clarifying moment the thought trickled through my mind that my child moving on in her life did not mean I had to be stuck in an old phase of mine. I had remade myself before, and now perhaps I might again consider new possibilities. Might my daughter's path be a transformational force that could teach me to travel a new road? Perhaps the time had come to pursue my dream of becoming an author.

As I stayed with my memories and their meanings, an ache in my psyche shifted. I felt as if an inner force was guiding me from the past into a new awareness of the present. I had known theoretically about the dual need for mothers and children to stay connected as well as to separate. Intellectually I had long understood that in order to achieve the highest potential of each, it is often necessary for parents and children to find separate paths that ideally will often cross. I began to understand more fully that "letting go" did not mean giving them up, but rather releasing them to follow the paths of their own individuality.

Feeling both the pangs of letting go and relief in the acceptance of what was, what is, and what might be, I recalled how my own mother had tried to mold me and hold me. Reflection on the ways her expectations often collided with my need to be true to my Self brought an awareness of my own intentions. What was important to me was supporting my girls to be authentically who they wanted to be, rather than expecting them to fit my image of woman, wife, or, someday, mother. I understood that as we three matured, being true to Self could actually keep us closer.

I promised myself that I would do my best to support my daughters in their own personal journeys. And I prayed that I would succeed in truly accepting, as well as being a part of, all the new stages in their lives. Honoring my intention to foster the highest good of us all, I psychically released my beloveds to their own choices and their own life paths, and affirmed that the connection between us could—and hopefully would—be everlasting. I would forever miss their baby-hoods, their childhoods, and our "just us-ness," yet I knew that even as life would present new roles to me—older mother, mother-in-law, and, blessedly, grandmother—I possessed the freedom to face the new requirements and rewards of my own life.

KEY STRATEGIES FOR PARENTING WITH SOUL WISDOM

When you are pressed, pooped, and perplexed, stress and emotional pain can block wise knowing. However, having a tool kit of strategies that combine your psychic intuition with best parenting practices and "uncommonly" common sense can move you from confusion to clarity. Over the years I have worked toward discovering what I consider to be key strategies for single mothers to parent with Soul Wisdom.

A balance of intuition and practicality together can lead to clearer solutions. My motto, "This, too, shall pass!" affirms that every moment morphs into the next regardless of whether it is a positive or a negative moment, and affirms the trust that problems can be dealt with and will fade. If you practice using sensible strategies and psychic guidance, you can release negative thoughts and improve your problem-solving skills. You might find it helpful to incorporate a daily or weekly personal practice of relaxation, meditation, or prayer to stay connected to your psychic knowing. You will find some ideas for this practice in chapters four and five.

As you read the following strategies, you may realize the ways in which they reflect your own solution-oriented choices, your intelligent intuition, and your uncommonly common sense. These tips assume that basic safety concerns for your children are being met in all circumstances. If a safety issue exists with one parent, the other parent is advised to seek legal and/or mental health counsel to determine the best way to minimize the stress.

You might like to use the "pages for journaling" at the end of this chapter to make your own list of key strategies, and assess the value and efficacy of the ones you choose to use.

Help your kids manage stress. It will reduce yours.

Children typically act out their stress. Stay alert for signs of stress that show up in behaviors. The intensity and amount of your child's stress will depend on age, development, temperament, and environment. Stress for children can arise from what they absorb in the domestic situation as well as from school, social, and internal sources.

Notice new behaviors that alert you to a new stressor. Excessive crying, difficulty sleeping, headaches, stomachaches, bedwetting, pushing limits more than usual, being physically aggressive, or acting in ways not typical to usual behavior may be signs of a child's stress. Pay attention to behaviors that deviate from the considered norm, and evaluate duration and intensity. Seek professional and/or medical help if the signs persist or worsen.

Manage your own stress. It will lower your children's.

Being a single parent causes high stress and often requires major adaptation to difficult circumstances. (Responsive-resilience!) Each of us has a typical coping style. Do you know yours?

Do you vent when you are stressed? Do you seek to be alone, or do you talk things over with a friend? Do you shut down, or do you eat, drink, and "be merry" a bit too much? Do you lose your appetite?

How you cope with stress will affect your kids. For instance, the stressed-out parent who stows away in her room will be less available to her children, possibly causing them to seek attention in negative ways.

Improve and develop your coping toolkit.

When the kids see their parent managing stress, their stress levels tend to go down. A child's stress can trend up or down in direct relation to their mother's effective coping. Spending a little time examining your own stress reactions can make a difference. Your children will notice what you say and what you do. They *will* use you as a model. The "Do as I say, not as I do" motto is a myth. The kids will "do as you do."

Refrain from releasing your stress onto your children either by displacing your frustration with harsher discipline or using the children as peer supports. Keep adult business in the adult world. Refrain from bad-mouthing the other parent in front of the children or to the children. Criticizing the other parent will hurt the kids and cause stress for everyone involved. You may not love—or like—your former partner, but the children are part of their other parent, or in some circumstances have been attached to a former non-biological partner of yours.

Do some self-esteem building.

Sense of Self can be compromised when you are separated and/ or divorcing, or even years into single motherhood. It's common for single mothers to question their Self worth when loss takes place, particularly if they have been in abusive relationships. But no other person can make you okay. You do not need a partner to be a whole person. You are worthy by virtue of just being.

Co-parent with the other parent as much as possible.

Co-parenting does not necessarily mean each former partner deals with the children exactly the same. But it's important for the kids that you do the best you can to keep lines of communication open regarding the welfare of the children. When appropriate and possible, co-parenting promotes less stress, is emotionally beneficial for the kids, and leads to better outcomes. If safety is assured, the co-parenting task is to put resentments and frustrations aside in order to talk about what is best for your kids. You have no control over how the other parent does this!

Open communication does not mean that you share your personal business or innermost feelings with your former partner, just that you actually do the business of raising the children and then let the kids know the practicalities and expectations of mutual or unilateral decisions.

Co-parenting may be easier said than done. Ironically, it might involve interacting with a former partner with whom communication was tough *inside* the relationship. However, co-parenting can potentially reduce the tension felt by the children, which is in their best interest and can go a long way to improving life for you.

Allow the children to stay connected to the other parent or former partner.

When safety is assured, allow the children to stay connected with the other parent (or former partner) and his/her family, when appropriate. However, refrain from using the children to find out what the other parent is doing, and as best you can, refrain from using the children as the liaisons for communication with the other parent, even though it might seem natural to do so. The more children are in the middle, the more stress and strain it puts on their developing psyches.

Keep open communication with your children.

Open communication with the kids means you explain what's going on at the level that they can understand. Do not give them adult detail. Do allow them to talk about what they did at the other parent's house, even if it's hard to hear. Refrain from criticizing the other parent, but address safety with him/her if needed. As best you can, offer the children opportunities to talk about their experiences and feelings without putting down the other parent.

Open communication *does not* include talking to the kids about your anger at their other parent or a former partner whom they loved. Your children may be biologically, psychologically, or emotionally attached to the other parent or a former surrogate parent. Because of this attachment a putdown of your "former" can be experienced by the child as a putdown of him or herself.

The less you burden your children with adult information, the less stress will be created for them, and probably for you, too. When the children are feeling less stressed, they are less likely to act out with inappropriate behaviors. Even if you have to crazy-glue your mouth, *do not put down the other parent, or former partner, to the kids or in front of the kids.*

Refrain from using your children as supports for adult business, but seek appropriate grownup support instead.

Ursula and I agree. Support is important enough to have a second mention. Support is especially essential for single parents. Seek groups, friends, and family members who can give you a hand, lend you an ear, or offer an hour to sit with the kids. Affirm for yourself that it is okay to ask, and learn how to do it with your head up. Remaking a good life means having people in it that you can rely on in a variety of circumstances. This might take some time and some effort, but it will go a long way to making life better.

Have fun with the kids.

This key is often overlooked because single parents are typically busy, overworked, and overtired. But having some fun is emotionally and physically important, and, based on new research, even neurologically important! Having positive time together can cement a sense of family and bonded connection. And it doesn't have to be expensive. If you can't take a vacation, take a few hours off on the weekend to play. You can take a walk, throw a ball, have a picnic, catch a Frisbee, or go to the local playground. You can also go to outdoor concerts in summer or sit and tell stories in winter.

In the age of high tech and almost constant texting, this may be a challenge. However, the sense of well-being created by having fun together can reduce everyone's stress, lessen the chances of kids' negative acting out to gain attention, and energize the feeling of having a good life that is so critically necessary to regain after separation and divorce.

Use a no-shame-no-blame approach to correcting behavior.

Respond rather than react to children's behavior. Shaming and blaming hurt a child's growing sense of Self worth, which can lead to other problems down the road. Ask questions, gather information if you can, and explain things to children in terms they can understand. I use the motto "Be Fair, Firm, and (emotionally) Flat." In other words, to the best of your ability keep your own high emotion from getting in the way, and do your best not to yell at the kids. Keeping your temper under control is one of the essential tools of Soul Mother Wisdom's parenting power. The less you react and overreact, the better traction you will get in your parenting success.

However, do use reasonable consequences that do not overreact and do not place a heavy burden on you to monitor. Smaller consequences can work well. The key feature here is *follow through!* Think carefully about saying "If you do ____, I will do ____," for if you *don't,* your leverage and authority may be on the line.

Use wisdom and sense regarding your home environment.

- Whatever the family dynamics, keep as much consistency and predictability in the children's lives, and your own, as you can.
- Children thrive in an environment of trust and stability. They need boundaries and need to know what the boundaries are. Children love you and will offer you their respect and forgiveness when there is a foundation of safety and trust.
- Establish routines that involve responsibilities for the children and have consequences that you can follow up on when needed. Kids learn to trust when you do what you say you will do.
- Keep your home environment reasonably stable and predictable within life's normal changes.
- Make no "house rules" that you cannot back up. In other words, refrain from using threats for disciplinary measures. If you do that and do not follow through, you lose credibility.
- Make sure the kids—and of course this varies with age levels—understand the idea that choices lead to consequences. The message is that they can be "the bosses of their own behavior." This provides them with a sense of control along with knowing you are in charge.
- If the other parent has a separate household, give the kids the message that what happens in that house isn't necessarily the same as what happens in your house. This can be tricky, especially if the other parent's rules are less strict or predictable, but still it matters to keep consistency in your own household.

Forgive yourself for being a single mother.

Some women feel guilty or ashamed for being a single mother in a world that values coupleness. Remember you are a whole person and your family is a whole family. Forgiving yourself for being a single parent is a component of Soul Wisdom. Forgiveness is a process that benefits your own peace of mind.

You might like to use the following exercise to release yourself from

Self-criticism and Self-blame:

> As I honor the spirit of my truth, I now release myself from blame. I am doing the best I can, and my best is good enough. My children are my greatest opportunity to practice being all I can be as a mother and as a woman. I parent from a place of increasing Self-wholeness, centered in forgiveness. I release anything disharmonious and focus my awareness on all that is loving, hopeful, and accepting.

Rely on Soul Mother Wisdom.

Develop your awareness of what you can and cannot control in any given situation. If you're like I was, you'll want to have just about everything in your control—even the weather. However, learning to let go of what you can't control will give you greater peace of mind.

Here are some prayers and mottos that have helped me to let go and let God. (You can replace g-o-d with g-o-o-d, if that works better for you.)

- Prayer for letting go: "All forces in the universe are working toward my higher good, and the good of all concerned."
- Motto for letting go: "If I turn something over to God (or "Good") without letting go, I will end up upside down."
- Prayer for letting go: "God/Good, please put your arm around my shoulder, and your hand over my mouth."
- Prayer for letting go: To your Higher Power: "Please let me not act crazy today."
- Motto for letting go: "This, too, shall pass."

TIPS FOR UNDERSTANDING:
PARENTING WITH SOUL WISDOM

You will be using Soul Wisdom when:
- You and the separating partner tell the kids together, when possible—even if one parent has left the home—about what they can expect regarding changes in routines at the beginning of a separation and as circumstances change. Children will have many questions regarding when they will be with you, how and when they will see friends and

extended families, and what life will be like. Information helps to reduce stress for everyone. Children will have less stress when they know what to expect.

- You avoid having one child know about a separation or divorce before the others and thus having to keep a secret.
- You jump out of the trap of anger, misery, and resentment by shifting your attention to what uplifts and comforts you. It can be as simple as looking at a beautiful flower or picturing a peaceful scene in your mind.
- You avoid resentment. Resentment is like taking poison and expecting someone else to get sick or die.
- You refrain from seeing yourself as a victim. Victim mentality will keep you angry and resentful, putting you at risk to show or tell those feelings to your children. When you free yourself from the tension of victim thinking, the greater will be your ability to focus on what is important for making life sweet.
- You let the children know, whether with the former parenting partner or alone, that you may not always have all the answers. You can let the children know that the parents will work things out and will tell the children the plans when they are formed. It is best for young children to have plans arranged for them. With older children, you may find that they have some strong opinions. You can remind them that the adults will consider their preferences, but "the adults are in charge."
- You comfort and support your children by assuring them that both parents will continue to love them, take care of them, and be involved in their lives when possible.
- You co-parent with the other parent, providing that safety needs are met. Co-parenting and consistency are best for children. It's also best to keep them out of the middle of decisions that belong in the parenting realm.
- You understand that you can discuss things with the other parent, but cannot control the rules in the other household. You can have the rules you want to have in your own household.
- You understand that the kids may have many questions beginning with "Why?" But you do not discuss money, debts, legal issues, sex, or other adult issues with your children. Instead, you can answer

"why" questions like this: "Because things happen in life and parents do not have all the answers all the time."

- You reassure the children that though there may be some problems that they do not fully understand, they did not cause the problems and they cannot solve them for the adults.
- You consult psychic intuitive wisdom when you need your Soul guidance, trusting that you will be advised by the best intentions of your authentic Self.

IDEAS FOR REFLECTION AND INSIGHT: SOUL MOTHER WISDOM CAN LIGHT YOUR PATH TO PEACE

As a Soul mother you now know that wisdom comes from a close connection to your authentic Self and the qualities of your true MRS. You now know how to use inner guidance as well as practical strategies as you face and resolve difficulties and build a healthy life for yourself and your family. Using your unique brand of Soul Wisdom, you now know how to cultivate the insights and strategies to become a more effective parent and a wiser woman.

Understanding your personal life path will help you make choices out of faith in your ability to take correct action. Though living daily in the material world of chores and demands may feel frustrating and overwhelming at times, using Soul Mother Wisdom to cultivate actions that stem from gratefulness and forgiveness can light a path to more effective parenting, less stressful living, and the realization of inner peace.

I have always found parenting wisdom in the words of Kahlil Gibran in his beloved book *The Prophet.*

Your children are not your children.
They are the sons and daughters of Life's longing for itself.
They come through you but not from you,
and though they are with you, yet they belong not to you.
You may give them your love but not your thoughts,
for they have their own thoughts.
You may house their bodies but not their souls,
for their souls dwell in the house of tomorrow, which you cannot
    visit, even in your dreams.

You may strive to be like them, but seek not to make them like
   you.
For life goes not backward nor tarries with yesterday.
You are the bows from which your children as living arrows are
   sent forth.

PAGES FOR JOURNALING:
SOUL-EMPOWERED PARENTING

Single mothers live in the world of demands and responsibilities.
Whether partnered, not partnered, or married—yes, even some married women parent alone!—you are doing the hardest job on the planet, and your story is amazing. Your personal story will reveal your inner spirit, the Self that knows what is best, and the MRS that supplies your unique brand of Soul Wisdom.

As you affirm the struggles, dreams, hopes, and successes, you can discover that you might be able to give yourself as much support and insight as any daily reader composed of someone else's wise words. As you enjoy the wisdom of your own personal story, you can find new ways to transcend the burdens and revel in the joys. You can create a personal chronicle that can sustain you for years to come.

You might want take a little time, now or any time, to reflect upon your Soul-empowered parenting triumphs, disappointments, aches, and longings, as well as your personal epiphanies, lessons and inspirations. Whatever comes to mind can be recorded in these Pages for Journaling. What you write will help reveal the power and meaning in your story, and support your everlasting connection to Soul Mother Wisdom.

INSIGHT SEVEN

Your Soul Sparkles with Gratefulness, Compassionate Forgiveness, and Outrageous Faith

"Me—Me—Me—I look in the mirror. Look within myself....A clear, pure, healing light illuminates me—swirls around me with glowing sparkles and shimmers—spiraling up from my feet and encircling me in ever-widening circles around my outstretched arms. Glittering on my fingertips as I slowly rise, floating as if in a calm sea. The light keeps going, right up over my head before it begins to dissipate. And still it keeps coming, rising up from the floor. Floating freely. Free of fear."

SINGLE MOTHER, CIRCA 2008

MY SOUL SPARKLES

It was long ago, on a summer day on Fountain Street, that I discovered the sweetness of my Soul's sparkle. I was four.

I lived with parents and maternal grandparents in a duplex owned by the Baretts. The Baretts' younger daughter was my best friend. I adored Marla. She always had a little spark of mischief up her sleeve, and I always went along for the ride. I also loved Rosie, Marla's big sister. Rosie's long red hair and 10-year-old grownupness intrigued me. My parents, my grandparents, and the Baretts made up a rich extended family for me. Across the hall from our apartment, Marla and Rosie's house seemed to bubble over with fun.

Outside there was fun, too. Out back of our big white house a large field grew, surrounded by what seemed to me like deep and mysterious woods. In the middle of the field, under an arbor, a large garden created the special secret world that little children love. Deep in the mystery of field and flowers, frolicking with the neighborhood kids, Marla and I played in a world of magic. How I loved those days.

As we ran in the tall grass Marla would sing, "Next to you Gravel Gertie woulda looked awright!" I had no idea what that meant, but Marla's impish delivery with her gentle lisp would make me giggle until I hurt. Sometimes Marla would find milkweed pods for us to blow into the air. She could spot the ones that had magical colors inside— blues, pinks, and yellows. I have never again seen milkweed pods like that, and I have often wondered, "Is it only children who can see those colors?"

That house, that field, and those woods had it all. The giggles, the songs, the pods, and the people inspired my first connection to my sparkle. It was in that magic, on a warm and brilliant summer day, that I first felt the joy of my inner light, and *knew* I had a Soul. Here is how it happened.

The two households, including four parents, my two grandparents, and Rosie and various other Baretts, were sitting on the back stoop chatting and watching the field where we little kids were doing our usual runaround. I was wearing a pinafore, the type of sundress I always felt special wearing, but this day the good feeling was new and different. I was excited and full of a happy lightness that carried me back and forth from field to stoop and back down into the garden.

Inside the arbor I gathered into my pinafore gobs of what I could not see. As I ran with each invisible bundle to my family on the steps I felt an indescribable exuberance, knowing in my just-past-baby consciousness that I was filling my skirt with love. Sensing intuitively that *it* was seeping from all that was alive in the woods, in the field, in the garden, and on the steps. I named *it* "energy," and in the delight of my discovery, I could not get enough or gather it fast enough.

Nor did I question its existence, for I had complete faith that this "energy" existed, and that whatever it was, it was endless. Each time I ran to plop a scoop in the lap of a loved one laughing on the steps I felt joy flowing from me to them. I flew, transported to a place of protection and peace for which there were no limits and no bounds. It was perfect, and I knew I was perfect. Filled with exquisite aliveness in the flow of all that is, I experienced an unquestioning acceptance of Self.

No fears or doubts crept in to destroy these sacred moments. I understood that with this sweet sparkle running through me I could do anything. Although it would be years before I would have words to comprehend or describe the wisdom of my experience on Fountain Street, the meaning and purpose of my life have formed around this event like a pearl.

YOUR SOUL SPARKLES

As adults with enormous responsibilities and often-overwhelming stress we can be pulled away from the radiance of the inner sparkle, but touching the true colors of your Self can be as simple as taking a deep breath and imagining the sparkling colors of a magical milkweed pod.

Single mothers particularly can benefit from a warm relationship with the energy of the inner being. Some of you already have had glimpses of this gift, and might like to experience more. Some of you may be curious about it, and looking forward to discovery.

For a moment, consider this: What life events can you recall that might have revealed your sparkle? Have you discovered contact with your inner spirit offers wise guidance when you face difficulties?

I have found that each experience of my sparkle is uniquely special, offering insight into a problem, understanding of a relationship, or comfort in a crisis. Each time I am guided by my inner spirit I have even greater faith that its wisdom will be available the next time I need it.

Now, I invite you to experience your own sparkling Soul space with the following exercise. You may return to this experience as many times as you wish.

Starting with a gentle breath, relax into a place of comfort that is right for you. As you breathe normally, you can begin to experience a certain sense, or an image, of luminosity that reflects the true nature of your sparkle.

Your sparkle might glitter brilliant colors, shimmer with pink, or radiate the orange light of a glowing sunset. Your sparkle might shine with the rainbows of the Northern Lights.

And you can imagine the infinite number of ways to be warmed and filled with the sparkling energy of unconditional love.

As you allow your sparkle to surround and fill your being, you can experience it with your senses, coming to a personal understanding of your sparkle. You can intuit what it feels like, looks like, sounds like, or even tastes like. In this way, getting to know the sparkling energy that dwells inside your inner being.

And now you can imagine that your sparkle has a voice—the voice of your Soul, filled with wisdom that can guide you with its truth and the inspiration to know what you need, even if you don't know exactly what that is. You can trust all the ways your sparkle is holding you, helping you, and healing you at your most essential level.

You might like to take a few moments to become more familiar with your sparkle. You can play with your sparkle—expanding, enlarging, coloring, or sending energy from it to others. If memories or thoughts come in, you can let go of them or let them be. You can trust that this experience can reenergize your resilience, revive your inspiration, and strengthen you for your journey.

You can affirm:

I trust the loving guidance of my sparkle. When I listen to the voice of my Soul my spirit sparkles with abundant joy, and I am guided into the wisdom of gratefulness, forgiveness and faith.

When you are ready, you can reorient back to your physical space, trusting that the inner spirit of your sparkle is the true source of Soul Mother Wisdom.

Keep in mind that your soul sparkles at any age, and in all circumstances. With patience, practice, and perseverance your inner spirit will provide comfort and wise guidance to light your path to peace of mind.

MY JOURNEY CONTINUES

Like most of us, I grew up to find that day-to-day realities are not always as uplifting as that special day on Fountain Street. Nevertheless, the wonder of finding my sparkle began a journey to seek and be guided by the truth inside my true Self. Important chapters of my story, spanning years of chance, choice, change, and crisis, illustrate the many ways in which I have found, lost, and rediscovered my sparkle, and the many ways my sparkle has continued to find me.

This part of my story began when I was seventeen and fell in love with Tommy. Some history might help you understand the significance of the "Tommy" chapter of my life story and the chapters that followed.

Before they immigrated to Haverhill, Massachusetts, my grandparents spent childhood years in Europe during the period of violent anti-Semitism in the early 20th century. Despite having witnessed and endured discrimination as children and adults, my grandparents spared the next generation from the poison of hatred. In fact, I received from my parents and my maternal grandmother two valuable, positive lessons. First, that all people have worth, and second, that your substance is about who you are as a person, not about wealth or status.

These messages, consistently and conscientiously delivered, implanted in me unquestioning acceptance of diversity, the truth of the worth of all beings, and a budding core of Self worth. Yet despite the fact that their humanitarian values had survived the horrors of the early and mid 1900s, I was to discover that a different residual had rooted in my family psyche. When I fell in love with Tommy during our last year of high school, I discovered that the psychological effects of personal and cultural trauma had infected my grandparents and my parents with fear.

Puppy love? True love? It didn't matter. Tommy wasn't Jewish, and my family wasn't far enough from Nazi terror—and my father wasn't far enough from his major nervous breakdown—to reconcile their fears with their values. My parents and maternal grandmother dreaded the possibility that I might marry Tommy, and did their best to keep me away from him.

But I loved Tommy. He was intelligent, insightful, and kind, and we shared values. He respected other people, and he had lofty goals for his education and his future—achieved—success. Tommy's friendship felt right, and added a sparkle to my life. Tommy helped me understand myself better, and our connection brought me joy.

But my parents and grandmother, who lived with us, adamantly objected. Their disapproval caused me to doubt my perceptions and emotions. I could not fathom how, after all they had taught me, they did not understand that Tommy's innate goodness had nothing to do with religion. The dissonance between what they were saying and what they had been teaching created conflict in my loyalties, and created confusion within my Self.

Where my love was concerned, I couldn't tell what was right and what was wrong. It would only be years later that their rationales would begin to make sense. Their reasoning, based on generations of discrimination and persecution, was too deep for my teenage mind to grasp. I doubt they fully understood it themselves.

Their reasons might have been buried in complexity, but their reasoning was open and simple. If I continued to "go with" Tommy, our family would be emotionally, socially, and financially ruined. My father would lose his business, have another breakdown, and worse, "this might kill him!"

I was confused, but I was also determined. I had been taught to see worth in others, to love. I knew Tommy was special, and despite protests and warnings I persisted. But now I had to lie about where I was going and about the friends I was with. In my attempts to remain true to my Self, various other truths split off from each other, once again fragmenting my Self-respect and my sense of Self.

My parents also persisted, however, desperately trying to influence me with threats of pending disaster and recriminations about my character. My father explained that this relationship was "just wrong" because he said so.

To make matters more difficult, Tommy's side also put pressure on us. A letter from Tommy's young priest explained that if we continued our relationship, Tommy would be ruined. Among his other absurd reasons Father Surrano stated that Tommy would not be able to go to college, and he would lose his religion.

Soon my world was upside down. Nothing made sense.

Tommy and I cared deeply for each other, but we also cared about our educations. We had been accepted to colleges, and Tommy was going to Holy Cross. But Father Surrano was the priest all our friends knew and trusted. I took his words to heart—he must know better. Still, how could I give Tommy up? He was my best friend. He understood my deepest feelings, helped me believe in myself, and—this was big—he knew how to help me with math.

I knew that what I shared with Tommy was good and true, but

another part of me knew that my relationship with him would eventually have to end. As the first two years of college unfolded, I realized that I wasn't strong enough to overcome the tide of guilt that continually washed over me. I didn't know how or when, but I knew someday I would have to give up my love or face dire consequences.

Despite our attempts to survive the waves of disapproval and doom coming from both families, the guilt was too much for me. I was drowning in Self-recrimination and shame, convinced that I was a destroyer with the power to cause my father to crack, maybe even to die. When Tommy went abroad at the beginning of junior year, I was devastated, but I saw my sad opportunity and wrote the "Dear Tommy" letter.

The next task was harder. I needed to freeze Tommy out of my heart or suffer from unbearable grief. For the last year and a half of college I threw myself into the party and dating scene, convinced that I no longer cared. I missed Tommy terribly, but the trade-off had benefits. I had given up Tommy for the relief of knowing that I had saved my family from disaster.

As the years would prove, not only was I unable to save my father from his mental illness, sadly, I had also lost contact with important parts of my Self.

When I cut off from Tommy, I dimmed a channel of connection to my sparkle. My connection to my authentic Self, having struggled so hard to prevail, was now unsure. I was oblivious to feeling abandoned by my parents, and numb to feeling betrayed by two religions that preached loving kindness.

I could no longer fully sense what was right for my life. Now I was like a piece of flotsam, floating this way and that, buffeted by the wind, easily able to be caught by any random item in its way. In my case that would be the next man whom I liked enough, thought I loved, and who fit my parents' requirements for—whose?—security. Dov could not have been a more perfect choice.

Dov was handsome, fun, smart, and popular. He had a funky antique sports car that he let me drive back and forth from Trinity College to the University of Massachusetts. But most important, he was Jewish. My parents approved of him and his family. There was no mention of the fact that I had just graduated, wasn't looking for a job, and was unprepared for adult life. I am not sure anyone noticed. I've always suspected that my parents were relieved that I would now be out of Tommy's reach.

After four months of dating Dov I got the diamond, and two months later, innocent, unseasoned and unsuspecting, with no clue about how to be one, I became a wife.

I believe that Dov and I did love each other, but I was not over being "in love" with Tommy. The summer that Dov and I were to be married I ran into Tommy. He told me he was going to marry a Catholic girl. I felt then what I know now was the grief I tried so hard to bury. But in the dimmed connection to my true Self I didn't understand what I felt, or how it might have guided me to a different choice. Now hope was truly gone for Tommy and me. He had chosen his path and I had chosen mine.

What I couldn't know then, and what took years to understand, was that by marrying Dov I had actually stepped onto my true Soul path, and had begun the long journey back to the inner wisdom of authentic Self.

But there was a lot to live through. Dov and I were unprepared for marriage. Though I was delighted to be part of both sides of my new extended family, I couldn't begin to foresee the emotional trouble we were heading into. No one could have predicted the crises and heartbreak to come, or the gratefulness and outrageous faith in Soul Wisdom that would someday break through.

THE WISDOM OF GRATEFULNESS

This next chapter of my life would continue into thirteen married years, two babies, separation, divorce, Dov's tragic death, and seventeen years raising my daughters on my own. Although for many years I believed I had been pushed into a wrong decision and a lot of hardship, a revised understanding of my story reveals all the ways my marriage to Dov, as well as my life as a single mother, redirected me back to my sparkle.

This is how the journey unfolded.

Dov and I settled close to a state teachers college. Since my undergraduate psychology degree had prepared me for virtually nothing, I entered the college's summer program to become an English teacher. For the next three months I lived, breathed, and wallowed in the delight of my student teacher education.

Living fully in the "now" of the experience, I had no idea of how I was doing academically—and I didn't much care. I had no idea that I would be named top student in the program. For the first time in years I was in the throes of being Me, and relishing the creative energy of true Self. Shortly after the program's completion I was hired to teach seventh and eighth grade English in a school headed by a true humanitarian. I will forever be grateful that Chauncey A., a young and visionary principal, believed in me and helped me once again to believe in my Self.

I discovered that being with my students brought me the same delight that student teaching had. I could feel the aliveness of my sparkle, and the exciting "rightness" of my work. With Chauncey as a mentor I flourished as a teacher and began to feel authentic again. The years I spent teaching began a re-growth of my Self-respect and the restoration of my wholeness.

However, in those days you had to stop teaching when a pregnancy began to show. Three years after I "retired" I was at home in a very married community north of Boston, caring for two precious babies and missing the fulfillment of a professional career. Fortunately in those days Dov and I could afford to pay fifty cents an hour for a babysitter, which allowed me to volunteer a few hours a week at the local counseling center and nearby Jewish Community Center.

Over the next few years, in those settings, I would enter therapy for the first time, deepen the gift of psychic ability, make a commitment to a new career, and begin to heal the old rift with religion. The skills, strengths, and insights gained during that time would serve me well in difficulties yet to come. Although I couldn't see it then, the life I had chosen with Dov, including the hard circumstances that followed, redirected me back to my sparkle and to the wisdom of my true Self as surely as a glacier can redirect a river.

The Wisdom of Compassionate Forgiveness

Years later, as a single mother, gratefulness would coalesce into acceptance of what was, appreciation for what is, and the wisdom to forgive. As I continued to heal from the ongoing traumas of divorce and Dov's death, I would come to understand the ways in which forgiveness that comes from compassion for Self and for the other could increase Soul Wisdom and brighten the light of my sparkle.

Understanding the fear my parents must have felt when they tried to prevent me from doing what they believed would ruin us all was one of my first experiences with compassionate forgiveness. Seeing me suffer after my separation, my mother asked my forgiveness for having pulled me away from Tommy.

Although I did forgive her then, my understanding of what compassionate forgiveness meant became clearer as wisdom grew. Just before she died, I forgave my mother again. This time my intention was to release *her* from any leftover guilt. This time I thanked her for having blocked me, and credited her with opening the way for my two daughters to be born and for my finding the purpose and fulfillment that has guided my life.

Forgiving my mother also meant having compassion for myself. In forgiving myself I could relieve regret for not having fought to marry Tommy and for choosing to marry and to divorce Dov. As a result, I could have faith that though life might have been different and good with other choices, the path I chose was right for me.

Still, there was much more for me to learn and experience about the wisdom of compassionate forgiveness. Jasper was instrumental in this important chapter of my life.

Intelligent, savvy and kind, Jasper was a piano player who loved music and loved me. He also loved my girls. Jasper's insightful support and dry wit added sparkle to my life. His devotion to my children helped keep us stable after Dov died. But unfortunately—and in some ways, fortunately—Jasper was also a functional alcoholic.

Although I was learning about the disease of alcoholism in social work school, I did not yet comprehend the stealth of its progression. In the beginning Jasper's drinking had not progressed to dysfunction, and for years our relationship was nurturing, grounding, and comforting. But as his drinking increased, Jasper became less physically and emotionally available. My Soul Wisdom knew the situation was deteriorating, but I remained in denial to the fact that Jasper was very sick.

When Jasper's dysfunction worsened to the point that I could no longer deny it, with deep sadness I ended our relationship. After eighteen months, we attempted to reconcile. Although our relationship was not to last, Jasper introduced me to a healing force that would last a lifetime.

During our time apart, Jasper had been going to AA. I became intrigued by what Jasper was telling me about the 12 Steps, and started going to meetings with Jasper and his sponsor. Although I had done my share of "partying" during the first two years of separation from Dov, and then from Jasper, I didn't think I was what Jasper and his sponsor called "a real one." But I recognized something powerful in the 12 Steps of Alcoholics Anonymous that I wanted. In 1991 I put down my last drink and dedicated myself to my own recovery, soon adding Alanon to my program to make me a "double winner."

Although it might seem outrageous, I am grateful to the disease of alcoholism. Through work with my Alanon sponsor, Rachel S., I was dealing with having given up Tommy, Dov and Jasper, and realizing that I was not a victim of those losses. For the first time I fathomed that forgiving those I had blamed could bring peace to me. My new faith in a Higher Power and Rachel's loving support were giving me a deeper understanding of compassionate forgiveness.

Another opportunity for compassionate forgiveness came in a most unexpected way.

Coincidentally—or not—a colleague in Boston, Sal Surrano, turned out to be the younger brother of Father Edward Surrano, the priest who had said Tommy would be ruined if we continued our relationship. Aware of my history both with his brother and with Tommy, Sal arranged for me to meet his brother at our Boston offices. Although my intent was to tell Father Surrano how his interference had "ruined" my life, the actuality of Soul Wisdom was a different story.

Father Surrano, having grown wiser himself, asked *me* to forgive *him!* Looking at the earnest gaze on his face, I realized the important opportunity being presented. From the perspective of making amends for having held him responsible for my loss, forgiveness came easily from compassion for his sadness.

I will always be grateful for the accuracy of chance that allowed this healing encounter to occur in Sal's office. As faith in inner knowing increases, you, too can become better able to recognize and intuit the variety of opportunities for compassionate forgiveness that can heal you and guide you to maturity, resilience, and strength.

A few years after Dov died, Soul Wisdom presented a different chance to experience yet another way compassionate forgiveness could provide inner peace.

A part of my psyche had harbored resentment toward my former in-laws since the time they had refused to help me keep our house. As my recovery advanced, it dawned on me that the only person directly affected by these awful feelings was myself. I also worried that holding this resentment might in some way indirectly affect my children. Soul Wisdom told me that letting go of this hurt was between me and my Self. I loved my former in-laws, and had no intention of hurting them by telling them how I was hurt. How, then, to rid my soul of this toxicity? Soul Wisdom once again answered the question. What I needed was a way to experience the felt sense of letting this resentment go. Once I knew this, the how-to came easily.

During those days my friend Joyce and I often took walks on the beach. With her trusted support and my faith in the potential for healing, we created a ritual designed to clear my heart of negativity and make space for compassionate and loving forgiveness.

On the chosen summer day, we stopped where the view of the ocean was most beautiful. There, with Joyce as my witness, I turned to the water and affirmed the many ways my former father-in-law and mother-in-law were actually offering support and help to my children. Once I spoke my gratefulness, I cast my resentment into the waves with a gesture and with these words:

"I cast anger and blame into the waves, where it will be healed and wash back to my heart with love. For those whom I love, I honor forgiveness as my true Soul nature. From this day on, whenever I think of them and the part they are of my life, I will realize only love. Every time my mind comes to this event, any negative feelings will wash away."

You may be wondering, "Did it work?" Although true enough, "yes, it did" is not a sufficient response. From that day I have rarely thought about that old hurt. Compassion for my former in-laws and for Dov's widow helped me realize they intended no harm. I believe they were unable to fathom the struggles I was facing, or how losing our home might have affected the children's stability. I believe they would never have done anything to hurt us, but in the midst of their own terrible grief they were taking care of business, doing their best to deal with what Dov had left behind. While I will always wish that they had understood my hardships, my compassion for the enormity of their loss, empathy for their pain, and motivation for my own healing inspired the forgiveness that unburdened my soul.

By forgiving my in-laws, I felt a surge in my own Self strength. I began to let go of feeling "less-than" and found compassionate forgiveness for being a single mother.

The time would come when I would also need to forgive myself for hurt I may have caused others in my attempts to rebuild my life. Two of those I hurt were Bethany and Darren, my former sister-in-law and brother-in-law, who grieved not only for the loss of Dov, but for the loss of me as a sister.

After my divorce and Dov's remarriage I could not find a comfortable place in the family I had loved. Because my own grief was so deep, and because I felt the need to make a new life, I created distance from them, which caused pain for my in-law siblings. However, it was crucial that the children remain close to their aunt and uncle, whom they loved and who were part of their vital connection to their father. Bethany and Darren's support of me and their generosity to my children, including many weekend trips away, helped me understand that despite their loss they held no resentment toward me. Their kindness to my children and consistent support for me helped me to forgive myself for any pain I caused them and for being the struggling single mother I was.

THE WISDOM OF OUTRAGEOUS FAITH

Can a stressed and overwhelmed single mother have faith that she will be okay? Can a frightened single mother believe that she doesn't have to be perfect to be a successful parent? "Yes, she can!" may seem outrageous, but believe it or not, "outrageous faith" in your ability to be wise, to be successful, and to be okay is possible to develop and practice. From a spiritual perspective, you can begin simply by believing that your Soul sparkles.

However, it might seem outrageous when you are exhausted, depressed, or in the midst of difficulties —which for many of us might be most of the time—to hold onto faith that you can manage painful emotions and overwhelming responsibility. In fact, why would a single mother not wonder, "How can I have any faith when my life is falling apart?" "How can I have faith when all I see is work, work, and more work?"

It might seem outrageous to ask a single mother to have faith that things will get better when she can barely see straight. But in fact, we are a resilient and capable lot.

In the midst of calamities, chaos, and confusion, having outrageous faith that a higher force is working for your highest good—which does not always mean working for exactly what you want—can help you muddle through. As Rachel S. taught me, it is possible to "walk in faith and not in fear" one day at a time. Practically speaking, "walking in faith" requires the willingness to switch gears on negativity and renew the trust in the invisible bundles of energy and love that are the essence of your Soul's sparkle.

However, let's be practical as well as a spiritual. Let's take a down-to-earth approach to cultivating the wisdom of outrageous faith.

First, the benefits of faith have been backed up by scientific information about the physiology and neurology of stress. Research now affirms what spiritual teachers—and psychics—have long known. *How* you think about *what* you think about has the power to affect your stress level, your emotional condition, as well as your physical health.

In 1988 an important *Newsweek* article announced, "New discoveries linking the brain to the immune system suggest that state of mind can affect us right down to our cells." It went on to discuss the mind-body connection, which we now understand to be biochemically as well as metaphysically real. It then dawned on me that this "new" information actually affirmed what I had been teaching in my "Stress Management through Psychic Development" classes! These "new" discoveries were actually part of a belief system that I was explaining to others. I was teaching my groups how to switch from negative to uplifting thoughts in order to relieve stress and nourish the inner being.

Might it be a good idea to practice what I was preaching? Yes, difficult things happen, but instead of worrying about what had happened and about what *might* happen, could I help myself by focusing on the attitudes and attributes that could give me courage to cope, and faith that the girls and I would be okay?

Shifting out of worry might take an outrageous amount of faith—

but it might be worth a try. I made a promise to my Self to stay more consistently connected to my inner wisdom. I wasn't perfect at it—no one is—but I worked at it. Still do! I found that I could change my thoughts to whatever would be more uplifting, and that it is possible, even in difficult circumstances, to develop a user friendly mind.

I practiced shifting my thoughts when anger, fear, or some other peace-of-mind stealer would set in. Often the switch was simple. All I needed was a meditation or a positive affirmation. Other times, when I needed more distraction, I might turn my attention to a book, some music, a good chuckle with a friend, or the comfort of reflecting on something one of the girls did or said.

I discovered that with faith you are able to be more peaceful. When you become more peaceful, you can develop even greater faith in your maturity, resilience, and Self-strength.

A passage from *The Millstone* by Margaret Drabble might help explain how "outrageous faith" can inspire the development of MRS and provide a window into Soul Mother Wisdom.

The central character of Drabble's book, Rosamund, an unmarried woman, becomes pregnant via unplanned and casual circumstances. During the pregnancy Rosamund becomes frightened as she attempts to fathom how to cope as a single mother.

Although she is alone, confused, and frightened, Rosamund's inner wisdom guides her decision to keep her baby. Rosamund develops faith that she is meant to have this child, and that its existence will give new meaning to her life. As the fetus grows, there is parallel growth in Rosamund's faith. Rosamund becomes a Soul mother even before her child is born. The following passage demonstrates the outrageous proportions of Rosamund's faith.

> The more I thought about it, the more convinced I became that my state must have some meaning, that it must, however haphazard and unexpected and masked, be connected to some sequence, to some significant development in my life....It was as though I was waiting for some link to be revealed to me that would make sense of connections though I had no evidence at all that it existed. At times I had a vague and complicated sense that this pregnancy had been sent to me in order to reveal to me a scheme of things totally different from the scheme which I inhabited...It was as though for too long I had been living in one

way, on one plane, and the way I had ignored had been forced thus abruptly and violently to assert itself.

Like Rosamund, even in the midst of troubled times it's possible to have outrageous faith that our circumstances, no matter how confusing or frightening, have meaning and importance. Rosamund used Self-talk to help herself find faith in her decision. In a similar way, you can practice talking to yourself and believing that events are working toward your highest good. One day at a time you can use this simple affirmation to practice outrageous faith:

All forces in the universe are now working toward my higher good and the good of my children. And this is so.

Whether your inner spirit is inspired by religion or by a secular belief system, you can come to believe in and rely on a higher source or being. Whether you name that source "God" or "Good" or "sparkle," your relationship to he, she or it can relieve your burden of stress and lift your spirit into a state of gratefulness, compassionate forgiveness, and/or outrageous faith. The peace that follows can provide access to the inner wisdom that knows what's right, and the courage to follow its guidance.

Esmeralda's story offers yet another example of the benefits of putting faith in the sparkle of Soul Mother Wisdom.

ESMERALDA'S SPARKLE

An engaging Latina, Esmeralda's spirit is as sparkling as her beauty. In our interview Esmeralda spoke of the way her dedication to her true Self led to her becoming a single mother.

Married to an uncommunicative and somewhat inflexible man whose introverted nature was in deep contrast to her outgoing, upbeat personality, Esmeralda found herself in a frustrating situation that became virtually unbearable when her son was born.

Now that she had become the mother she had always longed to be, Esmeralda experienced a restriction to her true nature. It felt to Esmeralda as if her husband's rigidity and his difficulty expressing emotions were constricting her natural exuberant expression of love for her son.

The awareness that in such an important way she was unable to live true to her Self led Esmeralda to a difficult life decision.

Realizing that she was no longer feeling flexible or joyful, and remembering her own childhood in which, despite an unfulfilling marriage, her parents stayed together "for the kids," motivated Esmeralda to divorce her husband. As she explained to me, "I had to be true to my Self."

When I spoke with her, Esmeralda had been a single parent for a couple of years, with physical custody and shared joint legal custody of her son. She told me that despite difficulty keeping perspective, she "feels great." She has created social supports and "up to a point" likes being a single mother.

After her marriage ended, Esmeralda had the wisdom to know that she could not replace her husband with her son. She also knew that for her child's benefit she would need to effectively co-parent with his father. As Esmeralda learned to manage life as a single mother, her love of life began to return.

Esmeralda realizes that being a single mother doesn't demand perfection, and in her wisdom she understands that how she parents her son and how she speaks to him about his father will affect his developing sense of Self and his emotional well-being. Esmeralda knows that how she has handled her huge life changes and what she believes about her courage and strength will allow her to continue to thrive.

Esmeralda tells her little boy how lucky they are—and she believes it. Her former husband has remarried, and Esmeralda makes a point of letting her son have a relationship with his father and stepmother uncontaminated by her past disappointments or current stressors. She tells me that she "goes to her inner wisdom" to know what's right for her and her son. Her intention is to keep him happy. And she understands that having a happy mother is part of what is healthy for him.

Esmeralda's inner sparkle surrounds her and extends to her little son, whose bright eyes reveal that he has inherited his wise Soul mother's beautiful and courageous inner spirit.

You, too can practice opening to guidance from the inner sparkle that knows what's best to think and to do. When you live inside your Soul's wisdom, gratefulness, forgiveness, and faith can flow throughout your entire being. Your spirit can wash off negative emotions and can connect you to a Higher Entity of your personal understanding.

You might try the following simple affirmation for healing emotional pain and connecting to your sparkle.

I encircle myself with sparkling light. I have faith that I am being divinely guided. Negative thoughts will have no ill effect on me. I allow only positive thoughts to affect me. Now loving energy washes off negative emotions, and I am filled with gratitude, resilience, faith, and the courage to go on.

IDEAS FOR REFLECTION AND INSIGHT: THE SPARKLING SOUL WISDOM INSIDE

The wise female characters in Margaret Zimmer Bradley's *The Mists of Avalon* transcend difficulties and fears using inner wisdom. They remind me that single mothers, too, are wise women. You can have faith that Soul Mother Wisdom is your soulmate, always by your side, helping you face life with the maturity of resilience and strength as well as the wisdom of gratefulness, forgiveness, and faith.

If you wish, you can use this exercise to find wisdom inside your true Self.

Imagine yourself in a beautiful setting—a garden, a meadow, a mountain, the woods, or a beach, or someplace out of this world that is just right for you.

Wherever you may be, see yourself moving toward mist in a vehicle of your creative imagination. As you get closer, see the mist lift, slowly or quickly, presenting a setting that is perfect for you. There, a beautiful, wise Lady waits to help you.

"My daughter, I am here to help. What would you request?"

Now, in the wise Lady's presence, you can ask for whatever guidance you desire, and you can realize the information or answers that arise in whatever way they come to you—words, pictures, or a general sense of something important that goes beyond words. Trust that you can have faith in what comes to you no matter how silly or outrageous it seems.

When you are ready, gently orient back to the outer dimension, bringing forth the tranquility of the inner level and your understanding of the wisdom you have received.

You can use the Pages for Journaling to write down what

meanings you ascribe to your Lady's guidance and how it can be helpful in your life.

TIPS FOR UNDERSTANDING: THE WISDOM OF YOUR SPARKLE

The Wisdom of Gratefulness

- Trust the gifts in, around, and underneath your problems, even though they may not be visible in the middle of a difficult situation.
- Reflect upon the ways in which a past problem eventually led to a positive outcome. Sometimes positive outcomes are readily understood, and sometimes they are subtle, requiring a new view.
- Revise the meanings in your story to see the ways in which an event that seemed unfortunate might have led to a positive outcome. New views can enhance the wisdom of gratefulness.
- Practice being grateful that you do not have to be perfect. You just have to be you, living true to your authentic Self, which is the essence of your sparkle.
- Consider making your own Gratefulness List. This works best when it doesn't feel forced or phony. List the things that delight you, bring you joy, elevate your optimism, and uplift your spirit, even if they seem silly or trivial. You may be surprised at what a true gratitude list can do for your sparkle.
- Cultivate gratefulness for the ways in which your children inspire you to grow and mature and to be the best (not perfect) single mother you can be.
- Feel the delight, joy, and aliveness in the experience of parenting your children as a single mother.

The Wisdom of Compassionate Forgiveness

- Forgiveness means mental and emotional relief for you from the emotional burdens of resentment and hostility. Consider this: Resentment is like taking poison and expecting someone else to die. Compassion for others can help you to move on.
- Discover that forgiveness can help you keep from concentrating more attention than necessary on your hurts and fears, thus allowing more mental and emotional space for uplifting thoughts and for quality relating to your kids.

- Give yourself the permission to disengage or discontinue a relationship when physical or emotional safety for you or your kids is at risk.
- Trust that the process of forgiving can reduce your stress and make you more available for the quality parenting you desire.
- Understand the process of forgiveness. Forgiveness is most effective when it includes validation for your pain and (as much as possible) compassion for the one who caused it. (Outrageous? Not when you understand that to forgive does not necessarily mean to excuse.) Even with a compassionate frame of mind, it's your right to discontinue a relationship, and when or if necessary employ legal help to support you.
- Forgiveness may include, but does not have to include, a dialogue with someone who has hurt you. Soul Wisdom can help you decide when the conversation is best between you and the other person, best between you and your therapist, or best between you and your Higher Power.
- Forgiving yourself for not being able to do it all, or do most of it perfectly, is your gift to your Self. It will allow the spirit within you to sparkle plenty.

The Wisdom of Outrageous Faith

- Practice believing that gifts and benefits exist in your problems. This type of "outrageous" faith can reduce your stress and release powerful forces in your Soul Mother Wisdom.
- Put faith in relaxation. Relaxation can connect you to your intuition and unlock the psychic ability that intersects with Soul Mother Wisdom.
- Trust that all forces are working for your higher good and the good of your children, especially in difficult times. This affirmation can lead to faith that could be called "outrageous."
- Put your faith in the strategies of strength and resilience as well as in a Higher Power (of your understanding). This trust can provide greater insight for parenting, as well as more peace and fulfillment for living.
- Consider reading *The Faith Factor* by noted cardiologist Herbert Benson, M.D., who also wrote *The Relaxation Response*. The findings of Benson's research can give an added boost to the faith that you

can heal yourself with the wondrous creativity and mental powers of your inner mind.

- Maintain the outrageous faith that Soul Mother Wisdom can affect your life in positive ways and can magnify the inner experience of your sparkle.

PAGES FOR JOURNALING
SEE AND FEEL YOUR SPARKLE

On these pages you might like to record the ways you see, feel, and experience your sparkle. You can also journal about the many ways gratefulness, compassionate forgiveness, and outrageous faith can heal you, enhance the beauty of your sparkle, and bring forth the magnificent results of Soul Mother Wisdom.

You can come back during a dark time, or any time you want to find inspiration in your own words. Your journal can build greater faith in your ability to be strong, to be resilient, to be gentle with yourself, and to trust that your Soul sparkles during all times.

Epilogue

Miraculously Empowered

Peace

Every day, it seems, someone says,
"Let there be an ocean bird
and let her reign."

I watch her swim through the air,
wrap her wings 'round the world.

Though aliens invade her shores,
ships, her seas

she dances with them.

She joins the rhythm
of the tides, the threat of rising waters,
frigid February winds
are her friends
as sultry ones of summer.

No need a change of feathers (a uniform?),
an order given
to prove she is someone.
No need to plunder,
throw rock, possess,
to prove her power.

In the quietness of her flight,
possession of herself.

No more than what she needs.
Peace.

MARYL WILLCOX, CIRCA 2010

It is a gift to your Self to remember that in the midst of the work-work-work of single motherhood there are experiences of insight, divine guidance, gratefulness, and faith that can seem like little miracles. Often I wonder if it's precisely because this path is difficult that it's so important to stay aware of these sacred opportunities for cultivating wise knowing and achieving inner peace.

In the middle of my divorce, such an opportunity—a moment of outrageous faith—presented itself. I saw that I could heal and succeed as a single mother, and that my girls and I could be okay. The powerful clarity of this insight gave me a felt sense of my solid inner core, and allowed me to believe that I could accomplish more than I ever dreamed I could.

Let me tell you how it happened.

One Friday evening after a particularly difficult "divorce" discussion, I was more distraught than usual. Since Dov had taken the children for the weekend, I was free to vent my emotions. I dropped to the floor of the little kitchen pantry and sobbed until I was limp. When my emotional tide receded I lay in the dark, not able to imagine how I would get up and go on.

During that stillness I prayed for relief from the anguish that I was feeling. I had no idea that my prayers would be so swiftly answered. Alone in the dark, with no tears left to weep, a little miracle occurred.

I felt a knowing come over me. A feeling in my core assured me I could go on. And "it" promised that we would be okay.

In that stunning moment, trust transcended pain. Slowly, conscious of the message, I felt newness inside. I knew I had received divine help. From that moment I had no doubt that I would not only survive, but that my children and I would thrive.

As you develop the qualities of Meta-maturity, Responsive-resilience and Self-strength, you will discover the infinite number of ways that you can receive and perceive intuitive guidance. With practice you will be able to transcend negative emotions and illuminate your spirit with the wisdom of your own inner sparkle.

As you continue to develop Soul Mother Wisdom, you will become ever more empowered to accomplish the tasks of single motherhood.

You will come to feel the rightness of your insights, and learn to recognize which strategies to use for more effective parenting and more fulfilling living.

YOU ARE NOW EMPOWERED TO ACCOMPLISH SEVEN CRITICAL TASKS

With a road map for your journey to wholeness and a toolkit of resources that belong to your true MRS, you have now become empowered, by the miracle of your wisdom, to accomplish seven of the most critical tasks of single motherhood.

Now you can:

1. Transform insecurities and fears into faith that you are whole.

In or out of a marriage, with or without a partner, your single-mother-headed household is not broken, but is an intact family in which all participate in making it work.

You now know that single mother families are real families. You know that while having a primary relationship is a healthy and valid goal, you have no need for another person to define you or complete you. Believing in your wholeness, you model for your kids that they are whole too, and that they come from a family that is intact. You understand that your positive Self-identity empowers not only you but also your children to have positive Self-regard as they develop their own maturity, resilience, and strength.

2. Take heart from the support and insights you derive from the stories of other single mothers.

As you talk heart-to-heart with other single mothers, read their stories, and think about your own life, you are able to realize how capable, strong and resilient you really are. You can now allow others' courage to remind you of your own strength, encourage you to to become more effective in your parenting, and inspire you to trust the wisdom of your authentic Self.

Now you know that your story and the stories of other single mothers reveal treasures of resilience and strength. Your courage and your successes inspire your parenting. As you add positive meaning to your story, you are able to see more fully the many ways in which you have experienced the wise guidance of your psychic knowing.

3. **Manage your stress and painful feelings while staying emotionally connected to your children,** because you understand that your Self-management helps them deal with their own stress, emotions, and behavior, and empowers their growing resilience and independence.

You now know that managing your own stress effectively has the potential to increase your peace of mind, improve your physical health, and bolster your emotional connection to your kids. You know that the more effectively you manage painful feelings, the greater the possibility for your children to manage theirs, which will lead to reduction in anxiety for all. You now understand that when parents model the ability to regulate feelings, and stress, kids are more apt to exhibit adaptive behaviors.

4. **Allow your children to remain connected to the other parent and extended family,** assuming safety needs are met. Because you understand that children identify with both parents and benefit from having relationships with both, you have the wisdom to refrain from preventing these relationships. Now you have strategies for managing any feelings of competition, insecurity, and/or resentment in order to keep from transmitting these negatives to your kids. When painful feelings do arise due to your children's connections with other people in their family, you know how to find peer outlets for coping. In such cases you also know that you can apply gratefulness and forgiveness to help you deal with your emotions.

5. **Refrain from using your children (even older ones) as emotional supports,** but rather seek appropriate adult/peer support for venting or for emotional working through.

Meta-maturity, which allows you to see the overview of situations, now informs you that using your children for emotional support puts too much pressure on them and can create conflicted loyalties that can confuse them. This applies even to older kids. Because, as always, you have their best interests at heart, you seek out peer and/or professional support for your own emotional needs.

6. Use a combination of inner wisdom, a toolkit of positive coping strategies, effective parenting skills, and outside supports to reason through problems and manage fears and insecurities. When you operate with these resources of Soul Mother Wisdom you increase the potential for protecting your children from excess stress.

Now your intuition, a strategy toolkit, and an outside support system come together as major coping resources for the dilemmas and problems of parenting and living. As you use your newly acquired tools, you are empowered to avoid many of the negative thoughts that steal your courage and bring you regret or fear. With gratefulness for your growth, you add substance to your maturity, resilience, and strength. And with greater peace and fulfillment, you direct your journey to the destination of wholeness.

7. Cope as follows:
   - View difficulties as opportunities.
   - Assess the effectiveness of coping choices, and accept personal responsibility, without blaming Self or others.
   - Discard coping strategies that no longer successfully solve your problems.
   - Try out new strategies, and seek professional help when you need it.

   You know now that in a cycle of growing into true MRS you are able to recognize the opportunities that come disguised as difficulties and choose courses of action that lead to successful solutions. As circumstances arise, you know how to discard strategies that do not work and try new ones that might be more effective. Rather than blaming yourself when things are rough, you have the wisdom and know-how to develop and to believe in positive Self-affirmations and solutions. You are now empowered to integrate Soul Mother Wisdom into the wholeness and authenticity of your bestest, truest Self.

Bonus Tips for Miraculous Empowerment

- Know your intentions, for they underlie your coping choices.
- Embrace your mistakes, for you can learn from all experiences.
- Keep life as stable and consistent as possible, for consistency encourages security.
- Don't be hard on yourself when life is hard, for it's okay (and advisable) to not be perfect!
- Learn and use stress management skills, for they will lead to more peace of mind for yourself and your children.
- Recognize your successes, for they will add positive meaning to your story.
- Believe that your authentic Self grows stronger every day—for it does.
- Take responsibility for your own actions without blaming others (or yourself), for doing so will promote forgiveness and gratefulness.
- Pursue activities and hobbies that make your life satisfying, for you deserve it.
- Practice coping strategies that work and discard the ones that don't, for you know how to recognize the ones that will be successful.
- Affirm that it's okay to have feelings, and attend to those aspects of life that uplift your thoughts, for this will heal your emotions and heighten the brilliance of your sparkle.

If you keep in mind the ideas and strategies of *Soul Mother Wisdom: Seven Insights for the Single Mother* even some of the time, you will increase your ability to accomplish not only these seven critical tasks, but also any task that single parenting requires. Single motherhood will always provide material for practicing the skills of MRS, and will always offer opportunities for recognizing and cultivating Wisdom.

PAGES FOR JOURNALING:
WITH ENCOURAGEMENT AND HOPE,
THE JOURNEY CONTINUES

As an authentic woman with an integrated, solid sense of Self, you now know how to keep your psychic channel open and keep your spirit sparkling.

You know the benefits of redirecting your perspectives from negative to positive, and your attitude from downhill to up.

When dealing with overlapping stressors, you know how to go inside, contact Soul Mother Wisdom, and trust your inner guidance to adjust your perspectives and make your decisions.

Now a path of enlightenment and understanding leads you to a destination of wholeness and true MRS.

You know now that no matter what rolls in, you can roll up your sleeves and know how to do what has to be done.

You have created a solid center of Self that can hold you together in peace even when you feel like you're going to pieces.

You now have a personal understanding of what being a single mother means to you.

May your journey continue with the powerful miracles of Soul Mothers' Wisdom.

About the Author

Bette J. Freedson, L.I.C.S.W., L.C.S.W., C.G.P. is a clinical social worker and certified group psychotherapist based in Southern Maine. She earned her master's degree in social work from the Boston University School of Social Work and a B.A. in psychology from the University of Massachusetts.

Throughout her career as a clinician in private practice, as well as a speaker and writer, Bette Freedson has worked with hundreds of children, parents, adults, couples, and groups to help them relieve the stress that interferes with success in life. The knowledge she has collected from years of experiences working with single mothers, as well as from her own personal experience as a single mother, has provided the material for *Soul Mothers' Wisdom: Seven Insights for the Single Mother.*

A sought-after speaker and media expert, Freedson has been featured on radio shows, websites and magazines including "Spiritually Speaking," "Start Feeling Better Now," Education.com, *Help Starts Here* (the consumer website for the National Association of Social Workers), *Woman's Day, Working Mother Magazine* and *Calgary's Child Magazine.*

Bette Freedson lives in South Berwick, ME with her husband. Visit her on the web at www.bettefreedson.com.

ABOUT PEARLSONG PRESS

Pearlsong Press is an independent publishing company dedicated to providing books and resources that entertain while expanding perspectives on the self and the world. The company was founded by Peggy Elam, Ph.D., a psychologist and journalist, in 2003.

We encourage you to enjoy other Pearlsong Press books, which you can purchase at www.pearlsong.com or your favorite bookstore. Keep up with us through our blog at www.pearlsongpress.com as we promote health, happiness and social justice at every size.

Healing the World One Book at a Time

FICTION

Heretics: A Love Story & *The Singing of Swans*—
novels about the divine feminine by Mary Saracino
Judith—an historical novel by Leslie Moïse
Fatropolis—a paranormal adventure by Tracey L. Thompson
The Falstaff Vampire Files, Bride of the Living Dead, Larger Than Death, Large Target, At Large & *A Ton of Trouble*—
paranormal adventure, romantic comedy & Josephine Fuller mysteries by Lynne Murray
The Season of Lost Children—a novel by Karen Blomain
Fallen Embers & *Blowing Embers*—Books 1 & 2
of The Embers Series, paranormal romance by Lauri J Owen
The Program & *The Fat Lady Sings*—suspense novel & young adult novels by Charlie Lovett
Syd Arthur—a novel by Ellen Frankel
Measure By Measure—a romantic romp with the fabulously fat by Rebecca Fox & William Sherman
FatLand & *FatLand: The Early Days*—Books 1 & 2 of
The FatLand Trilogy by Frannie Zellman

Romance Novels & Short Stories Featuring Big Beautiful Heroines

by Pat Ballard, the Queen of Rubenesque Romances:
ASAP Nanny | *Dangerous Love* | *The Best Man* | *Abigail's Revenge*
Dangerous Curves Ahead: Short Stories | *Wanted: One Groom*
Nobody's Perfect | *His Brother's Child* | *A Worthy Heir*
by Rebecca Brock—*The Giving Season*
& by Judy Bagshaw—*Kiss Me, Nate!* & *At Long Last, Love*

Nonfiction

Acceptable Prejudice? Fat, Rhetoric & Social Justice & *Talking Fat:*
Health vs. Persuasion in the War on Our Bodies
by Lonie McMichael, Ph.D.
Hiking the Pack Line: Moving from Grief to a Joyful Life
by Bonnie Shapbell
A Life Interrupted: Living with Brain Injury—
poetry by Louise Mathewson
ExtraOrdinary: An End of Life Story Without End—
memoir by Michele Tamaren & Michael Wittner
Love is the Thread: A Knitting Friendship by Leslie Moïse, Ph.D.
Fat Poets Speak: Voices of the Fat Poets' Society & *Fat Poets Speak 2:*
Living and Loving Fatly—Frannie Zellman, Ed.
Ten Steps to Loving Your Body (No Matter What Size You Are)
by Pat Ballard
Beyond Measure: A Memoir About Short Stature & Inner Growth
by Ellen Frankel
Taking Up Space: How Eating Well & Exercising Regularly Changed My
Life by Pattie Thomas, Ph.D. with Carl Wilkerson, M.B.A.
(foreword by Paul Campos, author of *The Obesity Myth*)
Off Kilter: A Woman's Journey to Peace with Scoliosis, Her Mother
& Her Polish Heritage—a memoir by Linda C. Wisniewski
Unconventional Means: The Dream Down Under—
a spiritual travelogue by Anne Richardson Williams
Splendid Seniors: Great Lives, Great Deeds—inspirational biographies
by Jack Adler